B+4

POWERS THAT MAKE US HUMAN

POWERS
THAT MAKE US
HUMAN

The Foundations of Medical Ethics

Edited by Kenneth Vaux

University of Illinois Press   *Urbana and Chicago*

© 1985 by the Board of Trustees of the University of Illinois
Manufactured in the United States of America
C 5 4 3 2 1

This book is printed on acid-free paper.

Library of Congress Cataloging in Publication Data

Main entry under title:

Powers that make us human.

Includes index.
1. Medical ethics—Addresses, essays, lectures.
2. Ethics—Addresses, essays, lectures.   I. Vaux,
Kenneth L., 1939 –   . [DNLM: 1. Ethics, Medical—essays.
2. Human Development—essays.   3. Morals—essays.
W50 P888]
R724.P67   1985   174.2   84 – 28028
ISBN 0-252-01187-2 (alk. paper)

Contents

Introduction

In recent years the search for normative criteria to be invoked when ethical decisions are required in medicine has generated much interest. The disciplines of law, sociology, psychology, and moral philosophy have approached the issues with great skill. An impressive literature analyzing the conflicting values and delineating the dynamics of decision making is available. When guidance for specific decisions is needed, one finds in the literature a paucity of answers, only questions. What should we decide, and why? Deafening silence ensues.

It is not that answers are not advanced in both public sector and academic arena. The raucous banter of the opinionated is all too much with us: the various media keep the issues alive. One recalls the words of W. B. Yeats: "The best lack all conviction and the worst are filled with passionate intensity." In a pluralistic society, however, to what shared normative values do we appeal in making ethical judgments? How do we ascertain whether aborting for sex selection—or using recombinant DNA technology to create oil spill-eating bugs—is "right" or "wrong"? We lack a carefully articulated standard of judgment. This need forces us to seek normative ethical assertions—to shape foundations of ethics.

The major research centers in medical ethics have set themselves to this task. The Hastings Center, for instance, has convened a working group on the "Foundations of Ethics." The Kennedy Institute of Bioethics has continued its program of appointing professors from the major normative schools of thought: Christian ethics (Protestant), moral theology (Roman Catholic), Judaism, Islam. To further this inquiry, the Program in Humanistic Studies at the University of Illinois Medical Center convened a symposium on medical ethics as its Distinguished Ethics Lectureship under the Davis Bequest. These papers served as a point of departure for the present volume.

The concept underlying our symposium was the search for foundations of ethics—not in some syncretism of ideas but within the essential being of the person. In recent years many scholars have seen ethics as an anthropological inquiry. Is truth about what it is to be human and what is required to sustain this unique essence to be found in the biological, sociocultural, rational, or spiritual dimensions of human life? Here we have asked a group of our most thoughtful philosophers of medicine to reflect on those dimensions of the person that might yield sources of moral insight. They sought to probe the essence of human nature to see if norms appropriate to ethics in general and to medical practice in particular were to be found there. Each explored the issue of ethics in the light of one controlling theme, one power or "virtue" common to human experience: mortality, honor, subsistence, feelings, reason, hope, virtue.

With a Teilhardian scheme in mind, we look at the biological substratum of human existence. Today evolutionary biologists are writing about morality. Aggression and altruism, territoriality and guarding one's genetic offspring, even hope and religion, it is argued, are biogenetic impulses. Leon Kass, a physician-philosopher, gathered much of biophilosophical thought together in what is titled an essay on *mortality* but is actually an essay on immortality. Kass asks if the drive for species perpetuation and genetic preservation and the quest for longevity are appropriate in light of biological, social, and philosophical wisdom. Drawing on Hebrew and Greek insight on aging and dying, Kass argues no, calling for what C. S. Lewis would term "true immortality" instead of Dr. Weston's indefinite and unlimited extension of ourselves.

In the same spirit William May examines how, in our culture, we respond to aging and the aged. It is not contempt or condescending benevolence that we are in danger of losing but that sense of just respect that might be called honor or veneration. Webster defines veneration as "the highest degree of respect and reverence; respect mingled with awe, the feeling or sentiment exacted by the dignity, wisdom and goodness of a person."

Ivan Illich applies his finely honed scalpel to the question of *sub-*

sistence as the moral mode of living. Health, or well-lived convivial existence, is not so much a process of overcoming boundaries, modifying human nature, extending the life-span, or manipulating human economy as it is living in freedom and justice. Health, says Illich, is the "social context of people's aliveness." He speaks of the way we make our life together, structuring our provision of goods to meet our needs, forming our societal work. Illich argues that we submerge perennial native wisdom, humanness, and virtue when we industrialize not only the technical but the human side of existence. Human freedom, justice, and fulfillment, indeed that constellation of virtues we call health or well-being, is for Illich shaped by the way we politically configure our common life.

Our attention then turns from the evolutionary and ecological fabric of human life to the powers intrinsic to the human organism. Willard Gaylin's essay on *feelings* shows the way in which the moral substance of a person's life is portrayed within the colorful range of his emotions. As the mind finds behavioral expression in feelings, the mind in some sense articulates our emotions. In discussing the emotions attendant to human sexuality, Gaylin shows how emotions and morals relate. Passion drives both *behind* present impulse into the realm of instinctive and *beyond* in love toward transcendence. Grief, shame, and guilt (and their correlates peace, joy, and hope) reach toward the moral realms of the demonic and the divine.

If morality is rooted in our instinctive and emotive acts, it is as surely rooted in our intellectual life. The history of ideas has most often argued that ethics are a function of human *reason*. Tristram Engelhardt's paper forcefully defends the notion that man is a rational animal and a rational soul. The very existence of human reason demands the ethical imperative: that is, to be human, persons must also be moral. Reason in persons justifies their defense from unethical assault.

If reason provides the ground for ethical capacity and defense, then two kinds of issues in medical ethics can be addressed fruitfully. On the one hand, moral judgments on abortion and termination of treatment for reason of cerebral death use reason as the determining criterion. On the other hand, discussions of ethical themes such as autonomy, informed consent, and patient freedom accent reason as the source of the doctrine of personal inviolability. This latter argument has led some, like Dr. John Lilly, to extend protection even to animals such as dolphins, in whom he finds the rudiments of intelligence like ours.

A close affinity exists between the papers of Engelhardt and Joseph Fletcher. Indeed, Engelhardt contends that he has moved toward Fletcher in his recent thought. Fletcher builds on the utilitarian tradition, particularly in its emphasis on a quantitative moral calculus. Man is distinguished, says Fletcher, by his ability to enhance and empower his compassion with reason. The finest flowering of moral reasoning is logical and even mathematical judgment. The weighing of risks and benefits to the few and the many is the most reliable touchstone between good and evil available to human persons and thus constitutes true *justice.*

The human activity of weighing outcomes and gauging ethical actions in terms of consequences is fashioned from the human powers of premonition, anticipation, prediction, and *hope.* My essay shows that the notion of man as a forward-leaning creature (one who thinks through problems, plans, and acts out of a sense of purposiveness) is in itself posited on a view of reality in which transcendence stands over against our life. The history of our culture both has fashioned us to see the world in a certain way and in turn has been fashioned by our many-faceted being. This history has infused into the spirit of western man a linear sense of time. It has generated a sense of God as a divine being who stands at the dawn and consummation of creation and history as well as at the background of nature. This history has given man, in Sir Thomas Browne's words, a "greed of life and repine at death" that in part constitute his moral energy. He resists what is, in the name of what could be.

Once civilization dawned in the ancient Near East, God was no longer confused with Nature. This theological history has evoked a unique moral structure in persons whose culture flows from Sumer, Israel, Greece, Rome, and Europe. It is a way of being that asks: Who am I? What does my life mean? Where am I going? What is the destiny of my community? In short, it is a morality based on possibility—what life is becoming. The ethic is eschatologic, or normative. Norms are brought into life from beyond life.

In the final essay of this volume Stanley Hauerwas addresses the issue of moral power as it emerges in community. He has taken the classical notion of *virtue* in its twofold meaning of power and excellence and has shown that virtue as a power is convivial by nature. It comes alive within a community of persons. Hauerwas convincingly argues that neither biologic (or emotive) necessity nor reason is the heartland of virtue. In community, human nature becomes history as it expresses value. In this discussion the full power of the natural, the rational, and the religious is realized in a synthetic concept of human character.

Together the essays span the range of viable ethical positions current today. No single essay finally completes the quest for certainty: that is, what is the nature and purpose of moral action? What can one believe and how should one act? As individuals, the writers undertake this journey into understanding using varied approaches. Still, and most important, the essayists are united in a common seriousness of inquiry, a common respect for the power of the human person to live justly, responsibly, and respectfully—to cultivate wisdom, to foster hope—to care for himself and others.

These essays, then, testify to the inherent powers, the virtue, of the human person. Illustrations and case studies are drawn from the field of medicine and health care. In these transactions one quickly moves beyond the superficial and pedestrian into the profound reaches of human life. As such, it is a realm that illumines the entire field of ethics, for "ethics" means simply the great normative ideas translated into concrete life situations. We have brought the best in ethical theory to confront this poignant sector of human experience. We have struggled for definition, for clarity, for precision, for a new synthetic understanding of the nature and purpose of moral action—and for renewed commitment to the "powers that make us human."

Thanks to my wife, Sara, and to Professor Bert Anson for their collaboration and support in this as in all my projects.

Kenneth L. Vaux
Chicago

If we are not only to identify but harness our powers, we must first struggle with the most problematic of our human characteristics, our mortality. Biomedical advances press us to question not primarily what length of life we wish but, rather, whether we should grope toward physical immortality at all. That very mortality which so frustrates us can spur us instead to recapture the fresh view of the world that children possess—thereby creating a buoyant immortality of spirit which cheats death of its coveted prize, our inner self.

MORTALITY

Leon Kass

Why should we wither? Why should we, the flower of the living kingdom, lose our youthful bloom and to go seed? Why should we grow old in body and in mind, losing our various powers, first gradually, then altogether in death? Aging, decay, and death have been inevitable, as necessary for us as for other animals and plants, from whom we are distinguished in this matter only by our awareness of this necessity. We *know* that we are, as the poet says, like the leaves that the wind scatters to the ground.

Recently, this necessity seems to have become something of a question, thanks to research into the phenomena of aging. Senescence, decay, and even our species-specific life span are now thought to be the result of biological processes at least in part genetically controlled, open to investigation, and in principle subject to human intervention and possible control. Slowing the processes of aging could yield powers to retard senescence, preserve youthfulness, and prolong life, perhaps indefinitely. Should these powers become available, "whether to wither" and "why" will become live questions.

These should be live questions even now. First, the project to control biological aging is already underway and is part of the mission of the new National Institute on Aging. Whether and how vigorously to pursue this project is thus already a matter of public policy and demands our most thoughtful deliberation. Second, the consequences of any success in the campaign against aging are likely to be massive,

7

affecting all our important social institutions and our fundamental beliefs and practices. No other area of present biomedical research promises such profound alterations of our way of life, not to say of our condition. Finally, as the objectives of this project are in many respects continuous with the objectives of modern medicine (i.e. longer life and better health), thought about this future—albeit somewhat futuristic—prospect may illuminate current practice and belief. Most important, we might become more thoughtful about our stance toward mortality and its implications for how to live. We might be moved to re-examine some of the basic assumptions on which we have been proceeding—for example, that everything possible should be done to make us healthier and more vigorous, that life should be prolonged and death postponed as long as possible, and that the ultimate goal of medical research is to help us live in health and vigor, indefinitely. It is especially for the sake of such self-understanding that we must consider "Whether to Wither and Why?"

Prospects for Retarding Aging

Some Preliminary Observations and Assumptions

1. *Aging*: the biological processes, distinct from disease, that make the body progressively less able to maintain itself and perform its various functions. Aging entails progressive changes involving a gradual decline in vigor, a gradual degeneration of bodily parts and functions, an increasing susceptibility to disease, and an increasing likelihood of death. These changes are thought to be governed by a built-in "biological clock" or clocks, whose rate is species-specific and genetically determined.

2. *Life span*: the biologically determined upper limit on longevity, different for different species, between ninety and one hundred years for human beings. This would be the life span of most of us in the absence of specific mortal diseases and fatal accidents. Thus this specific age represents a "biological wall" against further increases in longevity by improvements in medicine or our habits of life.

3. The biological clock and its midnight hour are probably linked; slowing the rate of aging could very well lead to a longer life span.

Most knowledgeable people agree that the rate of aging probably can be slowed, but how much slowing or lengthening of life span is theoretically possible or technically feasible is anybody's guess.

4. The processes of aging are extremely complex and variable. Very little is known about their causes or about how to retard them. Still, the many theories which have been advanced now stimulate a growing amount of research. Moreover, some researchers believe that methods to slow aging can be discovered empirically, in advance of a full understanding of the causes. Such research is also currently being pursued.

5. The primary biological effect of age-slowing technologies could vary considerably—from increases in vigor with no gain in longevity, to a longer life span with all stages prolonged, to longer life with a prolonged period of decline or with partial or uncoordinated increases in vigor(e.g., stronger joints but weaker memory)—and cannot now be predicted. Here assumed is what is held to be the most attractive prospect, an increase in life span with parallel increases in vigor—for ten to twenty years, but perhaps even longer. Also assumed is an anti-aging technology that is easy to administer, inexpensive, and not burdensome or distasteful to the users: that is, a technology that will be widely demanded and used.

All these observations and assumptions warrant critical examination of the evidence and much further discussion,[1] but they suffice to provide a plausible and concrete basis from which to approach our fundamental questions. And though one should not spend too much time deliberating about the impossible, one should not unduly encumber discussions of desirability with details of technique. Ends, not means, are being discussed.

Social Consequences

Aging research is pursued and supported by some who aspire to longer life for man, recognizing as they do that medicine's contributions to longevity have nearly reached their natural limit. As more fatal diseases and other causes of death are brought under control, more and more people are living out the natural human life span. But aging research is also pursued and encouraged by many more who hope that it will help to prevent or treat the infirmities, degenerations, and general loss of vigor that afflict the growing number of old people. These ailments are, in large part, the hitherto necessary price for the gift of longevity, a gift made possible by previous advances in hygiene, sanitation, medicine, and general living conditions. The benefits of success for individuals are obvious: who would not like to avoid or minimize for himself or his loved ones the burden of weakness, immobility, memory loss, and progressive blindness, deafness, and dementia? These burdens to individuals are also costly for society: loss of productivity and expensive medical and social services ensue. By reducing these losses and these costs, the community too would benefit from alleviating the handicaps and dependencies of the aged.

Yet this is a narrow view of the social implications of retarding aging. The elderly are related to us not only as nonproducing objects of care and expenditure; especially as they are fit and able, they participate in the complex network of functions, institutions, customs, and rituals that bind us all together. One cannot change the lot of one segment of the population without affecting this entire network of relations.

To begin with, what would be the effects on the size and distribution of the population? The percentages and number of people over age sixty-five continue to increase: in 1900 they were 4 percent, today nearly 12 percent of our population; in 1900 roughly 3 million and today roughly 23 million. How would still further increases in these numbers and percentages, or the growing numbers of nonagenarians and centenarians, affect work opportunities, retirement plans, new hiring and promotion, social security, housing patterns, cultural and social attitudes and beliefs, the status of traditions, the rate and acceptability of social change, the structure of family life, relations between the generations, or the locus of rule and authority in government, business, and the professions? Clearly these are very complex issues, affected not only by changing demographic patterns but also by social attitudes and practices relating these various matters to perceived stages of the life cycle, and also by our ability to anticipate and plan for, or at least to respond flexibly to, dislocations and strains. Still, even the most cursory examination of any of these matters suggests that the cumulative effect of the result of aggregated individual decisions for longer and more vigorous life could be highly disruptive and undesirable, even to the point that many individuals would be *sufficiently worse off* through most of their lives as to offset the benefits of better health afforded them near the end of life. Indeed, several people have predicted that retardation of aging will present a classic problem of the Tragedy of the Commons, in which genuine and sought-for gains to individuals are nullified or worse, *owing to the social consequences of granting them to everyone.*

As one example, consider employment. How will the large number of seventy-, eighty-, and ninety-year-olds occupy themselves? Less infirm, more vigorous, they will be less likely to accept being cut off from power, work, money, and a place in society, and it would seem, at first glance, to be even more reprehensible than it now is to push them out of the way. New opportunities and patterns for work or leisure would appear to be needed. Mandatory retirement could be delayed, permitting the old to remain active and permitting society to gain from the continued use of accumulated skills. But what about the numerous tedious, unrewarding, or degrading jobs? Would delaying retirement be desirable or attractive? Also, would not delayed retirement clog the promotional ladders and block opportunities for young people just starting out, raising obstacles to the ambitions and hopes of all, save for longer job security for those who have made it aboard?

The planned undertaking of second and third careers could provide alternatives to later retirement, but with few exceptions such opportunities would require re-education during mid-career, especially now that knowledge and skills needed for work are increasingly sophisticated and require more and more specialized education. These same educational requirements render difficult the development of new and rewarding uses of postretirement leisure, and it is far from clear that leisure is most fruitfully used when stacked up at the end of a life in which work is regarded as the main source of dignity. And, in any case, if the old are to be at leisure, the middle-aged will have to pay, a task they are unlikely to want to undertake, strapped as they are by the mounting costs of caring for their young. Indeed, a basic question we are already struggling with, and not well, is how to accommodate our growing elderly population in a society already greatly troubled by feelings of powerlessness, frustration, and alienation among the young. If people lived healthily to 100 or 120, if institutions were altered to meet their needs, we would likely have traded our problems of the aged for problems of youth. Retardation of aging could really mean prolongation of functional immaturity. Isolated not only from the top of the ladders of power but even from some of their lower rungs, supported by or even living with parents into their thirties or beyond, kept in a protracted sexually mature "adolescence," frustrated, disaffected, rebellious or apathetic—the picture is not so unfamiliar as to be difficult to complete.

Clearly, to avoid such strains and disasters, great changes in social patterns and institutions would be needed, changes unlikely to occur except through strong centralized planning. The coming of such centralized planning will have consequences of its own, not all of them attractive or desirable.

This is but the surface of only one of the myriad areas of concern. The implications for society will be immense. It boggles the mind to think of identifying all the problems, much less evaluating whether or not, on balance, we shall be better off. Some take a very gloomy view. One scientist colleague advised me to think of society as an organism, its individual members as cells. In this metaphor, unlimited prolongation of individual life would appear as a cancer eating away at the body politic, preventing new life and new growth—a matter to which we shall return. Still, one should stress that questions about *consequences* are always in large part empirical and cannot be assessed in advance, though it is none too early to begin to formulate the questions worth asking.[2] One thing is clear: the stakes are very high and the issues very complex—enough to make us suspect utopian promises, projected from shallow glances through narrow lenses.

Against all these concerns about social consequences, it will be argued that we would adjust to a world of longevity. We would figure out a way. This confidence rests on what seems to be good evidence: we have always adjusted in the past. Let us grant this point. Let us for now overlook the fact that adjustment does not necessarily yield a more desirable state of affairs, and that not all change is progress. Let us not try to show that *this* technologically induced change may produce unprecedented changes, for which the history of *past* adjustments to novelty is an irrelevant source of optimism. Let us accept the optimist's view: that longer life for individuals is an unqualified good; that we will, in due time, figure out a way to cope with the social consequences.

The Proper Life Span

How *much* longer life is an unqualified good for an individual? Ignoring now the possible harms flowing back to individuals from adverse social consequences, let us consider only the question "How much more life is good for us as individuals, other things being equal?" How much more life do we want, assuming it to be healthy and vigorous? Assuming that it were up to us to set the human life span, where would or should we set the limit, and why?

The simple answer is that no limit should be set. Life is good and death is bad. Therefore, the more life the better, provided, of course, that we remain fit and our friends do too.[3]

This answer has the virtues of clarity and honesty. But most public advocates of prolonging life by slowing aging deny such greediness. Immortality, or rather indefinite prolongation, is not their goal—it is, they say, out of the question (because they deem it impossible?). They hope instead for something reasonable: just a few more years.

How many years is reasonably few? Let us start with ten. Which of us would find unreasonable or unwelcome the addition of ten healthy and vigorous years to his or her life, years like those between ages thirty and forty? We could learn more, earn more, see more, do more. Maybe we should ask for five additional years? Or ten more? Why not fifteen, or twenty, or more?[4]

If we can't immediately land on the reasonable number of added years, perhaps we can locate the principle. What is the principle of reasonableness? Time needed for our plans and projects yet to be completed? Some multiple of the age of a generation, say, that we might live to see great-grandchildren fully grown? Some notion—traditional, natural, revealed—of the *proper* life span for a being *such as man*? We have no answer to this question. We do not even know how to choose among the principles for setting our new life span. The number of years chosen will have to be arbitrary, barring some revelation or discovery.

Under such circumstances, lacking a standard of reasonableness, we fall back on our wants and desires. Under our liberal regime, this means on the desires of the majority. Though what we desire is an empirical question, I suspect we know the answer: the attachment to life—or the fear of death—knows no limits, certainly not for most human beings. Again, it turns out that the simple answer is the best: we want to live and live, and not to die and not to wither. For most of us, especially under modern secular conditions in which more and more people believe that this is the only life they have, the desire to prolong the life span (even modestly) must be seen as expressing a desire never to grow old and die. However naive their counsel, those who propose immortality deserve credit: they honestly and shamelessly expose their desires.[5]

Some, of course, eschew *any* desire for longer life. They profess still more modest aims: adding not years to life but life to years. No increased life span, but only increased health, increased vigor, no decay. For them, the ideal life span would be our natural fourscore and ten, or if by reason of strength, fivescore, lived with full powers to the end, which would come rather suddenly, painlessly, at the maximal age.

This has much to recommend it. Who would not want to avoid senility, crippling arthritis, the need for hearing aids and dentures, and the degrading dependencies of old age? Yet leaving aside whether such goals are attainable without simultaneously pushing far back the midnight hour, one must wonder whether, in the absence of these degenerations, we could remain content to spurn longer life, whether we would not become still more disinclined to exit. Would not death become even more an affront? Would not the fear and loathing of death increase, in the absence of its antecedent harbingers? We could no longer comfort the widow by pointing out that her husband was delivered from his suffering. Death would always be untimely, unprepared, shocking.

Montaigne saw it clearly:

> I notice that in proportion as I sink into sickness, I naturally enter into a certain disdain for life. I find that I have much more trouble digesting this resolution when I am in health than when I have a fever. Inasmuch as I no longer cling so hard to the good things of life when I begin to lose the use and pleasure of them, I

come to view death with much less frightened eyes. This makes me hope that the farther I get from life and the nearer to death, the more easily I shall accept the exchange. . . . If we fell into such a change (decrepitude) suddenly, I don't think we could endure it. But when we are led by Nature's hand down a gentle and virtually imperceptible slope, bit by bit, one step at a time, she rolls us into this wretched state and makes us familiar with it; so that we find no shock when youth dies within us, which in essence and in truth is a harder death than the completed death of a languishing life or the death of old age; inasmuch as the leap is not so cruel from a painful life as from a sweet and flourishing life to a grievous and painful one.[6]

Withering is nature's preparation for death, both for the one who dies and for those who look upon him. We may wish to flee from it, perhaps, or seek to cover it over, but we must know the costs of doing so.

Of *what* will we die in that golden age of prolonged vigor? Perhaps there will be a new spate of diseases, as yet unknown. More likely, the unnatural or violent causes will get us, as they increasingly do: by auto, by pistol, by fire or drowning, by lightning or bombing, some through anger and some through mercy, and some by poison from their own hand. Should we wish to avoid spilling blood, or desire a clean technological solution, we could require that our drink from the fountain of youth be accompanied by the implantation into our mid-brains of an automatic self-destruction device, pre-set to go off at an unknown time some eighty or one hundred years hence.

But to return from these macabre speculations to the main point: it is highly likely that *either* a modest prolongation of life with vigor *or* a preservation of youthfulness with no increase in longevity would make death even less acceptable and would exacerbate the desire to keep pushing it further away—unless, for some reason, such life should also prove to be less satisfying.

Could longer, healthier life be less satisfying? How could it be, if life is good and death is bad? Perhaps the simple view is in error. Perhaps mortality is not simply an evil; perhaps it is even a blessing—not only for the welfare of the community *but even for us as individuals.* How could this be?

The Virtues of Mortality

Most would agree that there is no virtue in the death of a child or a young adult—or the untimely or premature death of anyone—before he has attained to the measure of man's day. Indeed, I am not implying that there is virtue in the particular *event* of death for anyone. Nor am I suggesting that separation through death is ever anything but pain for the survivors, those for whom the deceased was an integral part of their lives. Nor have I forgotten that, at whatever age, the process of dying can be painful and degrading, smelly and mean—though we now have powerful means to reduce at least much of the physical agony. Rather, my question concerns our finitude and mortality as such, i.e., *that we must die,* the fact that a full life for human beings has a biological, built-in limit, one that has evolved as part of our nature. Is this fact also a virtue? Is our finitude good for us *as individuals?* (I discuss this question entirely in the realm of natural reason, and apart from any question about a life after death.)

To praise mortality—especially to doctors and nurses in the halls of a great medical center—must seem madness. If mortality is a blessing, it is surely not widely regarded as such. Life seeks to live and rightly suspects all counsels of finitude. "Better to be a slave on earth than the king over all the dead," says Achilles in Hades to the visiting Odysseus, in apparent regret for his prior choice of the short but glorious life.[7] Moreover, though some cultures—like Eskimo—can instruct and moderate somewhat the lust for life, ours give it free rein, beginning with a political philosophy founded on the fear of violent death and on the mastery of nature for the relief of man's estate, and reaching to our current cults of youth and novelty, the cosmetic replastering of the wrinkles of age, and the widespread—and not wholly irrational—anxiety about disease and survival. Finally, the virtues of finitude—if there are any—may never be widely appreciated in any age or culture, if appreciation depends on a certain wisdom, if wisdom requires a certain detachment from the love of oneself and one's own, and if the possibility of detachment is given only to the few. Still, if it is wisdom, the rest of us should harken, for we may learn something of value for ourselves.

It is awkward and perhaps improper for a relatively young man to

praise mortality, especially before his elders. Doubtless he will address people who are close to death, who may indeed know that they
or a loved one is dying, and his remarks may give offense or may appear insensitive. Moreover, because of the apparent remoteness of
his own end of days, he may simply not know what he is talking
about. If wisdom comes through suffering, perhaps only among the
old can there be wisdom about mortality. This may be indeed true
but whether this answer be right or wrong, the question is certainly
worth thinking about.

First, consider the problem of *boredom* and *tedium*. If the life
span were increased, say by twenty years, would the pleasures of
life increase proportionately? Would professional tennis players
really enjoy playing 25 percent more games of tennis? Would the
Don Juans of this world feel better having seduced 1,250 women
rather than 1,000? Having experienced the joys and tribulations
of bringing up a family until the last left for college, how many
parents would like to extend the experience by another ten years?
Similarly, those who derive their satisfaction from progressing
up the career ladder might well ask what there would be to do for
fifteen years after one had become president of General Motors or
had been chairman of the House Ways and Means Committee for
a quarter of a century. Did Velazquez get as much pleasure paint-
ing his 200th countess as he did his 150th? Even less clear are the
additions to personal happiness from more of the same of the less
pleasant and fulfilling activities that so many of us engage in so
much of the time. It seems to be as the poet says: "We move and
ever spend our lives amid the same things, and not by any length
of life is any new pleasure hammered out."[8]

A second question concerns *seriousness*. Could life be serious or
meaningful without the limit of mortality? Is not the limit on our
time the ground of our taking life seriously and living it passion-
ately? To know and feel that one goes around only once, and that the
deadline is not out of sight, is for many people the necessary spur to
the pursuit of something worthwhile. To number our days is the
condition for making them count, and to treasure and appreciate all
that life brings. Homer's immortals, for all their eternal beauty and
youthfulness, live shallow and rather frivolous lives, their passions
only transiently engaged. Indeed, they lived as spectators of the mor-

tals, who by comparision had depth, aspiration, genuine feeling and a real center to their lives. Mortality makes life matter, and not only in the chemist's sense.

There may be some activities, especially in some human beings, that do not require finitude as a spur. A powerful desire for understanding can do without external proddings, let alone one related to our mortality; as there is never too much time to learn and understand, longer and more vigorous life might be simply a boon. The best sorts of friendship, too, seem capable of indefinite growth, especially when growth is somehow tied to learning—though whether real friendship doesn't depend somehow on the shared perceptions of a common fate is a good question. But in any case these may be among the rare exceptions. For most activities, and for most of us, it is crucial that we recognize and feel the force of not having world enough and time.

A third matter is *beauty*. Death, says the poet, is the mother of beauty.[9] What he means is not easy to say. Perhaps he means that only a mortal being, aware of his mortality and the transience and vulnerability of all natural things, is moved to make beautiful artifacts: objects that will last; objects whose order will be immune to decay as their maker is not; beautiful objects that will bespeak and beautify a world that needs beautification; beautiful objects for other mortal beings who cannot create such themselves but who carry a taste for the beautiful, a taste perhaps connected to awareness of the ugliness of decay.

Perhaps the poet means natural beauty as well, which beauty—unlike that of objects of art—depends upon its *im*permanence. Does the beauty of flowers depend upon their fragility? Does the beauty of spring warblers depend upon the fall drabness that precedes and follows? What about the fading, late-afternoon winter light or the spreading sunset? In general, is change necessary to the beautiful? That is, is the beautiful necessarily fleeting, a peak that cannot be sustained? Or does the poet perhaps mean *not* that the beautiful is beautiful because mortal, but that our appreciation of its beauty depends on our appreciation of mortality—in us and in the beautiful? Does not love swell before the beautiful precisely on recognition that it (and we) will not always be?[10] It seems too extreme to say that mortality is the cause of beauty and the worth of things, yet it may be the cause of our enhanced *appreciation* of the beautiful and the worthy, and of our treasuring and loving them.

Finally, there is the matter of that particularly human beauty, the beauty of *character*, of *virtue*, of *moral excellence*. To be mortal means that it is possible to give one's life, not only in one moment, perhaps on the field of battle—though that excellence is nowadays improperly despised—but also in the many other ways in which we are able in action to rise above attachment to survival. Through moral courage, endurance of soul, generosity, devotion to justice — in acts great and small—we rise above our mere creatureliness, for the sake of the noble and the good. We free ourselves from fear, from bodily pleasures, or from attachments to wealth — all largely connected with survival—and in doing virtuous deeds overcome the weight of our neediness; yet for this nobility, vulnerability and mortality are the necessary conditions. The immortals cannot be noble.

Of this too the poets teach. Odysseus, long suffering, has already heard Achilles' testimony in praise of life when he is offered immortal life by the nymph Calypso. She is a beautiful goddess, attractive, kind, yielding; she sings sweetly and weaves on a golden loom; her island is well ordered and lovely, free of hardships and suffering. Says the poet, "Even a god who came into that place would have admired what he saw, the heart delighted within him." Yet Odysseus turns down the offer to be lord of her household and immortal:

> Goddess and queen, do not be angry with me. I myself know that all you say is true and that circumspect Penelope can never match the impression you make for beauty and stature. She is mortal, after all, and you are immortal and ageless. But even so, what I want and all my days I pine for is to go back to my house and see the day of my homecoming. And if some god batters me far out on the wine-blue water, I will endure it, keeping a stubborn spirit inside me, for already, I have suffered much and done hard work on the waves and in the fighting.[11]

To suffer, to endure, to trouble oneself for the sake of home, family, and genuine friendship is truly to live and is the clear choice of this exemplary mortal. This choice is both the mark of his excellence and the basis for the visible display of his excellences in deeds both noble and just. Immortality is a kind of oblivion—like death itself.[12]

Longings for Immortality

Perhaps if we lived indefinitely, we would need no commitment, seriousness, beauty, or virtue. We would be altogether different beings, perhaps capable of other satisfactions and achievements—though God only knows what they would be. And if mortality were such a blessing, why do so few cultures recognize it as such? Why do so many teach the promise of life after death, or something eternal, or something imperishable? We must face this challenge, for it leads us to the very heart of the question about mortality and our stance toward it.

What is the meaning of this concern with immortality? We are interested here not in the theological question but in the anthropological one: why do we seek immortality? Why do we want to live longer or forever? Is it really first and most because we do not want to die, because we do not want to leave this embodied life on earth or give up our earthly pastimes, because we want to see more and do more? This may be what we say, but it is not what we mean. Mortality as such is *not* our defect, nor bodily immortality our goal. Rather, mortality is at most a pointer, a derivative manifestation, an accompaniment of some deeper deficiency. That so many cultures speak of a promise of immortality and eternity suggests, first of all, a certain truth about the human soul: the human soul yearns for, longs for, some condition or goal toward which our earthly activities are directed but which cannot be attained during our earthly life. Our soul's reach exceeds our grasp; it seeks more continuance; it reaches for something beyond us, something that for the most part eludes us. True happiness, a genuine fulfillment of the deepest longings of our soul, is not in our power, and cannot be fully attained, much less commanded. Our distress with mortality derives from the conflict between the transcendent longings of the soul and the all-too-finite powers and fleshly concerns of the body.

What is it that we lack and long for? Many of our poets and philosophers have tried to tell us. Let us listen to a few.

One possibility is completion in another person. In Plato's *Sym-*

posium, the comic poet Aristophanes speaks of the tragedy of human
love and its unfulfillable aspiration. You may recall how we are said
to spend our lives searching for our own complement, our own other
half, from whom we have been separated since Zeus cleaved our
original nature in half:

> When one of them—whether he be a boy-lover or a lover of any
> other sort—happens on his own particular half, the two of them
> are wondrously thrilled with friendship and intimacy and love,
> and are hardly to be induced, as it is said, to leave each other's
> side for a single moment. These are they who continue together
> throughout life, though they could not even say what they
> would have of one another. No one could imagine this to be the
> mere sexual connexion, or that such alone could be the reason
> why each rejoices in the other's company with so eager a zest:
> obviously *the soul of each is wishing for something else that it
> cannot express, only divining and darkly hinting what it
> wishes.* Suppose that, as they lay together Haphaestus should
> come and stand over them, and showing his implements should
> ask: "What is it, good mortals, that you would have of one
> another?"—and suppose that in their perplexity he asked them
> again: "Do you desire to be joined in the closest possible union,
> so that you shall not be divided by night or by day? If that is your
> craving, I am ready to fuse and weld you together as a single
> piece, that from being two you may be made one, that so long as
> you live, the pair of you, being as one, may share a single life;
> and that when you die you also in Hades younder *be one* instead
> of two, having shared a single death. Bethink yourselves if this is
> your heart's desire and if you will be quite contented with this
> lot." Not one on hearing this, we are sure, would demur to it or
> would be found wishing for anything else: Each would unreserv-
> edly deem that he had been offered just what he was yearning for
> all the time, namely to be joined and fused with his beloved that
> the two might be made one. For this is the cause, that our an-
> cient nature was this way and we were wholes: to the desire and
> pursuit of the whole, then, we give the name *eros*.[13]

In a second account Plato's Socrates both agrees and disagrees with
Aristophanes. He agrees that we long for wholeness and complete-
ness but not in bodily union. Rather, love is the soul's longing for the
noetic vision, i.e., for the sight of the beautiful truth about the
whole. Our soul aspires most to be completed by knowledge, by un-

derstanding, by wisdom; only by possessing such wisdom about the whole can we truly come to ourselves, can we be truly happy. Yet Plato, too, strongly hints that wisdom is not given to human beings, at least in this life: *philosophia*, yes, the love and pursuit of wisdom, yes, but its possession, no.

The Bible also teaches of human aspiration. Once we dwelt in the presence of God, the source of all goodness and righteousness; now we are estranged. That separation from God's presence occurred as the immediate result of eating of the tree of knowledge of good and evil. The serpent promised that "your eyes shall be opened and you shall be as God," but "their eyes were opened and they saw that they were naked." No, we are not as God; we are naked, weak, not self-sufficient, possessed by powerful and rebellious desires that we can neither master nor satisfy alone. We are ashamed before ourselves, and we hide from God—even before we are caught and punished and well before we are blocked from the possibility of tasting of the tree of life. The expulsion from the Garden merely ratifies our estrangement from God and testifies to our insufficiency, of which our accompanying mortality is but a visible sign—or perhaps even God's gift to put an end to our sad awareness of deficiency.

The decisive facts about these and many other accounts of human aspiration are the following: (1) Man longs not so much for deathlessness as for wholeness, wisdom, goodness. (2) This longing cannot be satisfied fully in our embodied earthly life—the only life, by natural reason, we know we have. Hence the attractiveness of a promise of a different and thereby fulfilling life hereafter. We are in principle unfulfilled and unfulfillable in earthly life, though *human* happiness, i.e., that semblance of complete happiness of which we *are* capable, lies in pursuing that completion to the full extent of our powers. (3) Death itself, mortality, is not the defect but a mark of that defect. From these facts the decisive inference is this: *This longing—any of these longings—cannot be answered by prolonging earthly life. No amount of more of the same will satisfy our own deepest aspirations.*

Even the Christian promise of the end of days, which entails a resurrection of the body, is not to be understood as the beginning of a never-ending and greatly eased earthly life of the sort we know, an uninterrupted gala of wining and dining, of winters in the Bahamas and summers on the Riviera, of disco dancing in golden slippers and Super Bowls on the heavenly turf, or listening to Elvis Presley or Caruso, of playing ball with Babe Ruth or making love to Marilyn Monroe. The kingdon of heaven is a promise of redemption, of purity, of wholeness in the presence of love and holiness.

If this is correct, then the proper meaning of the taste for immortality, for the imperishable and eternal, is not a taste that the conquest of aging would satisfy: we would still be incomplete; we would still lack wisdom; we would still lack God's presence; we would still lack purity. If our eyes were opened, we would see that we were still naked. If not, we would continue our vain pursuits, probably not even knowing their vanity, in most cases unaware of what it is we want.

Perpetuation

Perhaps this is all a mistake. Perhaps there is no such longing of the soul. Perhaps there is no soul. Certainly modern biology doesn't speak about the soul, nor does medicine, nor do even our healers of the soul, our psychiatrists. Perhaps we are just animals, complex ones to be sure, but animals nonetheless, content just to *be here*, frightened in the face of danger, avoiding pain, seeking pleasure.

Curiously, however, biology has its own view of our nature and its inclinations. Biology also teaches about transcendence, though it eschews talk about the soul. Much as it acknowledges and delineates our capabilities and instincts for self-preservation and our remarkable powers to restore and maintain our wholeness, biology teaches us how our life points beyond itself — to our offspring, to our community, to our species. Man, like the other animals, is built for reproduction. Man, more than other animals, is also built for sociality. And man, alone among the animals, is built for culture—not only through capacities to transmit and receive skills and techniques but also through capacities for shared beliefs, opinions, rituals, traditions. The origins of these powers for culture and their significance are matters of dispute, but their existence is not.

Many have called attention to man's remarkable biological characteristics that prepare him for culture, including the following:

(1) *the prolonged period of neonatal yet still embryonic dependence and development,* called by Portmann the period in the social womb, during which the child learns to speak and stand and begins to perform voluntary actions; (2) *the upright posture,* which permits a beholding of the world that in turn elicits our curiosity, which exposes things at a distance and at the same time frees the hands to fashion means for overcoming distance, which brings us face to face with our fellows, opposed but in communication; (3) *our capacity for speech,* requiring special laryngeal and respiratory, as well as cerebral, development, and a relation to others with whom that capacity is actualized through a learned language; (4) *a sense of time* and powers of forethought for the future; (5) *special social passions,* such as friendliness, shame, pity, and respect, which permit and are cultivated in community; and (6) *special ethical powers,* including a capacity for acquiring a sense of responsibility, of fairness and concern for posterity, which culture requires but also nurtures.

To be sure, the present orthodoxy in sociobiology treats our sociality as but a fancy mechanism geared to the sole end of the survival of the human gene pool. A richer sociobiology might come to understand that it is not just survival, but survival of what, which matters. It might again remember that sociality and culture, admittedly part of the means of preservation, are also part of the end for which we seek to preserve ourselves, and that only in community and through culture do we come into our own as that most special animal. But however this may be, biology teaches that we must see ourselves as species-directed, not merely self-directed. We are built with leanings toward and capacities for perpetuation. (Aristophanes, in a speech that sought to defend homosexuality, conveniently forgot about procreation.) Is it not possible that aging and mortality are part of this construction, and that the rate of aging and the life span have been selected for their usefulness to the task of perpetuation? Could not overturning the process of aging place a great strain on our nature, jeopardizing our project and depriving us of success? For, interestingly, perpetuation is a goal that *is* attainable. Here is transcendence of self that is largely realizable. Here is a form of participation in the enduring that is open to us, without qualification—provided, that is, that we remain open to *it.*

Biological consequences aside, simply to covet a prolonged life span for ourselves is both a sign and a cause of our failure to open ourselves to this purpose. The desire to prolong youthfulness is not only a childish desire to eat one's life and keep it; it is also an expression of a childish and narcissistic wish incompatible with devotion to posterity. It seeks an endless present, isolated from anything truly eternal and severed from any true continuity with past and future. It is in principle hostile to children, because children, those who come after, are those who will take one's place: they are life's answer to mortality, and their presence in one's house is a constant reminder that one no longer belongs to the frontier generation.

The death of a child is a terrible thing: terrible because of the pain and suffering of both child and parents in his dying, terrible because of the lost opportunity for growth, accomplishment, and experience. It is especially terrible, and especially for the parents, because of a break in transmission, the loss of a link in the chain, the loss of potential accomplishment both for the child and the parents. For the perpetuation we send forth not just the seed of our bodies but also a bearer of our hopes and truths, and those of our tradition. If human beings are to flower, we need to sow them well and nurture them, then cultivate them as seedlings in rich and wholesome soil, clothe them in fine and decent opinions and mores, and direct them toward the highest light, to stand straight and tall—that they may take our place as we took that of those who planted us and who made way for us, so that in time they too may plant and make way. But if we are to truly flower, we must go to seed, to sow and wither and give ground.

However, to seek immortality through one's children can be a snare and a delusion, perhaps today more than ever. Continuity of lineage, and more importantly of mores and beliefs, is in no way assured, not least because our ethos has become less hospitable to the concern for transmission, in our effort to push back our own deaths and ensure our private rights to the endless pursuit of happiness, understood as end-less pursuit. But there is something that we can certainly preserve and perpetuate, and only through sowing fresh seed. To see this, we need to look again at the nature of growing old.

Those who look primarily at the aging of the body and those who look upon the social and cultural aspects of aging forget a crucial third aspect: the psychological effects simply of the passage of time, i.e., of experiencing and learning about the way things are. After a while, no matter how healthy we are, no matter how respected and well placed we are socially, most of us cease to look upon the world with fresh eyes. Little surprises us, nothing shocks us, righteous indignation at injustice dies out. We have seen it all already, seen it all. And our ambition, or at least our noblest ambitions, begin to flag. At some point most of us turn and say to our intimates, "Is this all there is?" and we settle, we accept our situation—if we are lucky enough to have been prepared to accept it. In many ways, perhaps in the most profound ways, most of us go to sleep long before our deaths. In the young, aspiration, freshness, and openness spring anew, even if and when they take the form of overturning our monuments. Immortality for oneself through children may be a delusion, but participating in the natural and *eternal* renewal of human possibility through children is not—even in today's world.

For it still stands as it did when Homer made Glaukos say to Diomedes:

"As is the generation of leaves, so is that of humanity. The wind scatters the leaves to the ground, but the live timber burgeons with leaves again in the season of spring returning. So one generation of man will grow while another dies."[14]

May it always be so.

NOTES

---

1. See *Assessing Biomedical Technologies: An Inquiry into the Nature of the Process*, ch. IV, "Retardation of Aging," prepared in 1973 by the Committee on the Life Sciences and Social Policy of the National Research Council— National Academy of Sciences, and reprinted in 1977 by the National Science Foundation from whom it is now available. See also *Extending the Human Life Span: Social Policy and Social Ethics*, ed. Bernice L. Neugarten and Robert J. Havighurst, a report prepared for the National Science Foundation, RANN-Research Applications Directorate (NSF/RA 770123), available from U.S. Government Printing Office, Washington, D.C. 20402, Stock No. 038-000-00337-2.

2. See "Retardation of Aging."

3. These qualifications are, of course, crucial. Jonathan Swift's satirization of the wish for immortality depends on the fact that his immortal Struldbrugs (*Gulliver's Travels*, Voyage to Laputa) outlived all their contem-

poraries and became senile and decrepit. He thus failed to present the best case for immortality.

4. One is reminded of the perhaps apocryphal story about Samuel Gompers, who once gave testimony at a trial involving alleged Communist infiltration into the labor movement. The attorney for the defense cross-examined Mr. Gompers:

"Mr. Gompers, can you tell the Court, what is the goal of the American labor movement?"

"Very simple," said Gompers, "in one word: More."

"And when you have achieved more, what will be your goal then, Mr. Gompers?"

"More."

"And after that, then what?"

"More."

At which point the attorney addressed the bench:

"You see, your honor, the American labor movement is far more radical that the Communist Party. We only want everything."

5. See, e.g., Alan Harrington, *The Immortalist* (New York: Avon, 1969).

6. From "That to philosophize is to learn to die," *The Complete Essays of Montaigne*, tr. Donald M. Frame (Stanford, Calif.: Stanford University Press, 1965), p. 63.

7. *Odyssey*, XI, 489; tr. Richmond Lattimore (New York: Harper & Row, 1965).

8. Lucretius, *De rerum natura*, III, 1080; tr. Cyril Bailey (Oxford: Oxford University Press, 1947), p. 359.

9. Wallace Stevens, "Sunday Morning," in *The Collected Poems of Wallace Stevens* (New York: Knopf, 1955), pp. 66-70.

10. Shakespeare, Sonnet 73:

"This thou perceiv'st, which makes thy love more strong,

To love that well which thou must leave ere long."

11. *Odyssey*, V, 215-24, pp. 93-94.

12. The name Calypso means "one who hides or conceals or covers over."

13. Plato, *Symposium*, 192B8-193A1; tr. W.R.M. Lamb, Loeb Classical Library (Cambridge, Mass.: Harvard University Press, 1925), pp. 143-45.

14. *Iliad*, VI, 146-50; tr. Richmond Lattimore (Chicago: University of Chicago Press, 1951), p. 157.

Even when mortality, the brand of our humanity, can be accepted with grace and hope, our aging is difficult to accept and endure. The biomedical advances that have extended the years of many have confused our attitudes toward the old person: honor, once deemed a "natural" human response to aging, has been disturbed by economics, politics, crowding, and uncertainty. We need new ways in which we, as human persons, can recapture that honor which properly is due the aged, growing from the more general respect and concern that bind us to one another.

HONOR

William May

Until recently, dying was not a peculiar specialty of the aged, for people died at any time. Indeed, childhood was the most perilous of times, far more so than old age: the cradle was closer to the grave than the rocking chair. More people died in infancy than survived it. Many women died in childbirth and both men and women died from infections while in the full flood tide of life. Death was not automatically linked with advancing years. In one sense, the aged were peculiarly distanced from death. They had passed beyond the perils of infancy, the uncertainties of childhood; they had weathered the ills that plagued their juniors. They were the survivors, those who had won in the struggle for life in a world beset by death: the feisty farmer, the rugged granny, the daunting man of letters— the Sigmund Freuds and the George Bernard Shaws—women who presided over salons, and old pirates, the Rockefellers and Fords, who commanded fortunes. One did not even need to be a successful old man or woman to be respected. To reach old age was itself a rarity and, therefore, a kind of success, a performance. The aged few were venerated.

In our own time, however, there has occurred what the statisticians call a squaring of the mortality curve. The vast majority of people live seven decades. Recent projections suggest eighty-five or so as a natural life span. For the first time in history, becoming old is commonplace. This fact, as much as any other, accounts for the failure in America to honor the aged in our time. They are no longer a rarity.

Decline of respect for the aged, however, has many additional causes. The response particularly tempts an immigrant, perpetually migrant, pragmatic, secular, and proudly independent people. An immigrant country distances itself from forebears. Coming to America itself entailed a kind of abandonment of the aged: it meant leaving the old country, the land of one's forebears, for a strange land, often without the comfort of one's mother tongue. Immigrants made an extraordinary sacrifice and placed an equally extraordinary pressure on their sons and daughters. In Great Britain, W. H. Auden once said, children are under pressure to live up to their parents, but in America, until the 1950s, parents expected their children to outstrip them. This compulsion to surpass one's parents meant in turn that an immigrant people became a perpetually migrant people. Children left home for college—their first step into the middle class—in quest of better jobs than their fathers and of better homes and kitchens than their mothers had. They spilled out of the cities into the suburbs and across the land, hoping to improve their lot, leaving their elders behind or seeing them off to those huge territorial nursing homes of Florida and Arizona.

Americans, further, are a pragmatic and functional people. They tend to locate their identity in their doing rather than their being. People stripped of their work forfeit their identity. They lose their self-respect and therefore their hold on the respect of others. For the ruling generation, the aged slip into the margins of consciousness. In this regard America has been called the most secular of countries—not in the general religious sense of that term but in its original reference to those who orient their lives to the *current* generation, the generation that holds the power and exercises the authority. This insight may come closer to the root of things than the conventional characterization of America as a "youth culture." A consumerist society is secular in the sense that it orients with a vengeance to the current generation. It squanders the resources of the generations to come and distances itself from the heritage of generations past. In abortion it deals ruthlessly with the dependent young, and, in the nursing home, somewhat shabbily with the dependent old, all of this mostly for the sake of the generation now in charge.

But the neglect to which secularism leads does not tell the whole story. To the degree that the aged increase in numbers, they actively threaten the generation in charge. This occurs partly through an increase in political power. The elderly have become a power block: they have already influenced legislation and court decisions; they have reacquired the right to work beyond sixty-five, reclaiming their identity through doing; and through Medicare, Medicaid, and cost-of-living adjustments in Social Security, they have protected their identity through their holdings. The elderly currently get $150 billion out of the annual federal budget, and by the year 2040, it has been predicted,[1] some 20 per cent of the total population will be elderly, with 40 per cent of the federal budget devoted to their care. We may be moving rapidly from neglect into a period of resentment and hostility toward the aged.

That hostility, moreover, may go much deeper than resentment toward the political power of the aged. We are dealing with something new in the world: a vanguard horde of the elderly, a massive group that may increase still further with the development of life-extending technologies. We do not yet know what threats, psychological and otherwise, this population shift will pose for middle-aged adults, who are not used to having their elders around for long. At one end, the middle-aged have lengthening responsibilities for dependent youths (adolescence now seems to go on forever). At the other end, the middle-aged have worries about those who linger indeterminately in their dotage. Middle-aged adults are chiefly responsible for order and provision—they become embattled fortresses—while the young and the old seem to indulge themselves in an endless state of transition and dependency.

Still deeper than the external burden is an internal threat the aged pose to their adult children. As Ronald Blythe put it, the middle-aged

> frequently find themselves timidly yet compulsively, like tonguing a tooth nerve—measuring their assets against those of youth to see what they have left, and against those of old age to see what has to go. It is often a great deal in both cases. There can be then a spiritual and physical drawing back from the old, as if they possessed some centrifugal force to drag the no longer young into their slipstream of decay.[2]

The aged remind the middle-aged of their own imminent destiny.

What the middle-aged fear, however, is not merely physical decay, the loss of beauty and the failure of vitality, but the humiliation of dependency. Americans have always taken pride in themselves as an independent people, beholden to none for political institutions, economic resources, and personal choices. The dark side of this aspiration to self-reliance is an abhorrence of dependency. To depend upon others makes us angry, frustrated; it humiliates us at the deepest levels of our being. Philip Slater once observed that Puerto Ricans stranded in New England for the winter found more than the climate cold. The Yankee traditions of independence shut them off from spontaneous help from others as they knew it in their own culture, where to be dependent was not to sink below the level of respect.[3] This American compulsion to be independent enlarges the threat of old age, a threat which no person can avoid, since, as we are relentlessly told, the elderly are one minority which every one of us joins.

What strategies have we adopted for the care of the aged and what further clues do these strategies offer us about the American character and ideals? First, the strategy of sequestering. We respond to the aged as we would to any other great challenge from a neglected minority: we designate them as a cause and mobilize professional services to address their needs and develop large institutions to accomodate those in extreme old age. The difficulty with this strategy is that it impoverishes with the same stroke that it attempts to aid. We sense this impoverishment in the very design of the buildings to which we consign the elderly. Most nursing homes architecturally mock the word "home." What "home" contains 60 to 160 people in a cinder-block impersonality of space, classifying inmates according to the level of services they require and declassifying them again for common activities dominated by recreational interests of those of the lowest common denominator? These are neither homes nor surrogates for homes. The aged dread entering there. Like dogs that tremble as they are about to be left at the veterinarian's, the aged shiver at the thought of their permanent consignment to a nursing home. We know, moreover, of the assault that this change of life sometimes makes upon memory and therefore competence. Consider the man in his eighties who turns off the gas jet seven or eight times after preparing his breakfast. He has enough memory left to know that he should do it, but not enough left to know whether he has done it. But if you deny that man enough supplementary services to sustain him in familiar surroundings and if you relocate him in a large institution with its architectural accommodation to staff rather than residents, then his memory and competence precipitously deteriorate. While we sequester in part to maintain our own independence from the aged, we increase their dependency.

This stategy of distancing ourselves from the aged by placing them in the hands of professionals and by sequestering them in large institutions reflects our pattern of treatment of other deviant groups—the sick, the defective, the delinquent, and the insane. We subject them to a kind of premature burial. Inmates become what a prisoner once called "the forgotten men." We used to say: children should be seen but not heard. Institutionalization has become a way of saying to the aged: you should be neither seen nor heard.

Our reasons for segregating the aged do not spring entirely from ruthlessness or complacency. The nuclear family is already overloaded; adult children work; the home seems too small to accommodate. People already feel pressed to the limit of their resources. If we examine our reasons for institutionalizing, we discover not callousness but anxiety, not self-assurance but harassment, not riches but emotional bankruptcy. The question "But what could I do?" is often but a way of saying in despair, "I have nothing for the real needs of another because I cannot satisfy my own. What help could I possibly be to him? Better to avoid him. To have to face her would be too depressing. He would remind me of the emptiness of my own fate." We remove from sight the maimed, the disfigured, the retarded, and the decrepit because we have already condemned to oblivion a portion of ourselves. To address them in their needs would require us to permit ourselves to be addressed in our own needs. For some such reason it is preferable, even at great expense, to have them removed from sight. And what better way to place them in the shadows and obscure our own neediness than to put them in the hands of professionals whose *métier* it is to make a show of strength, experience, and competence in handling a given platoon of the distressed? Thus the exigent and aged are converted into an occasion in and through which the community seeks to exhibit its precedence and power over them.[4]

When the character of a people highly prizes self-sufficiency and independence, it has a difficult time allowing the negative and defective to surface—especially in oneself and therefore in others. The link between these two areas in which we repress the negative becomes clear if we consider converse efforts to let the negative surface. The liturgical traditions of Christendom include prayers of both intercession and confession. They relentlessly insist that the church pull to the center of its consciousness those whom it is tempted to push off to the margins—the sick, the aged, the dying, the imprisoned, the distressed. Equally important, the Christian life includes prayers of confession, which provide an important psychological basis for the humanitarian concerns of prayers of intercession. Michael Foucault observed in *Madness and Civilization*[5] that medieval society was much less inclined than the modern world to incarcerate its own members for reasons of deviancy. Medieval folk let the mad and the indigent mingle in the society at large. But by the eighteenth century the idle, the poor, the insane, and the criminal were increasingly locked away in huge institutions of which our twentieth-century nursing home for the aged is an extension. Foucault believes that the prayer of confession was important in shaping the more humane medieval attitude toward deviancy. Confession assumes human weakness and imperfection, but it also implies some confidence that the negative in human life can be let out into the open without engulfing those who vent the negative in prayer. After the seventeenth century western society felt increasingly "ashamed in the presence of the inhuman." It assumed that one could handle evil only by banishing it. An age that aspires to human autonomy and independence finds it more difficult to admit into its life the dependent, the defective, the deformed, and the irrational. They represent a negativity so threatening and absolute that they can only be put out of sight. At least ideally, confession invites a person to acknowledge weakness and fault in himself and thus allows him to address the distress of others. Confession makes possible intercession and service to others.

Philanthropy: The Ethics of the Self-Sufficent Giver

The moral ideal of philanthropy coordinates with the personal ideal of self-sufficiency. It is an ethic of love without ties. It rejects the notion of common identity and mutual dependency. It presupposes sufficiency and independence on one side and needy dependence on the other. Philanthropy shapes the moral ideal of professionals and amateurs alike in the United States. It is chiefly an ethic of giving, but it is not without spiritual dangers. As an ethic, it presupposes a great divide between the two parties to a transaction: giver and receiver. Ronald Blythe neatly dissects the problem:

> One of the fateful developments in the consciousness of many old people is that, in the eyes of the society, they have become another species. Ironically, an intensive caring and concern for their welfare is frequently more likely to suggest this relegation than indifference or neglect.[6]

> In the past a young man looked at an old man and said, "It is myself," and shuddered. In the present, a young man will look at an old man and say, "He is my brother," and help. Self-detachment allows him to participate in things which would be unendurable to the self-identifying. This helping of the brother who can in no way be oneself has become a cult. It may bring old persons some comfort, but it also makes them uneasy.[7]

> The old person being visited knows that he is simply being visited. He knows that he is in receipt of a charitable act and that this is no true relationship.[8]

The old do not want outreach; they want association.[9] The ideal of philanthropy that informs the care of the aged reflects the moral ideals to which Americans generally and the Protestant churches in particular have been committed. The Protestant social ethic, whether in its evangelical or liberal phase, has been almost obsessively and exclusively an ethic of love, an ethic of giving. The mark of the Christian life is disposability and responsiveness to the plight of the neighbor. Christians in this favored land are called upon to be generous to those outside the circle of their good fortune. Whites should be generous to blacks, Americans to the Third World, lawyers to their clients, teachers to their students, parents to their children, the healthy to the stricken, the middle-aged to the aged, and so it goes, the outward procession of love.[10] Americans defined themselves out of the human race, and the American church out of Chris-

tendom, when they presumed that they were the exclusive specialists in philanthropy, serving others from a promontory above them.

Similarly, members of the helping professions have been inclined
to define themselves by their giving alone—with others indebted to
them. The young professional identifies himself with his competence; he becomes a self-sufficient monad, unspecified by human
need, while others appear before him in their neediness, exposing to
him their illnesses, their crimes, their ignorance, or their advanced
age, for which the professional — as doctor, lawyer, social worker,
nurse, minister, or teacher—offers remedy.

The very words we apply to the professional and to the client reflect a power imbalance in the relationship. The lawyer is advocate,
that is, the one who *speaks for* his client. The client is the person
who literally *audits*, that is, who needs a mouthpiece on his behalf.
The word "patient" similarly denotes passivity. One is triply passive: to the ravages of disease, to the heroics of the professional, and
to the aggressive action of drugs, knife, and burning iron in the body.
Similarly, the student, at least conventionally understood, occupies
a position of somewhat demeaning inferiority and dependency. He is
eager, zealous, at the feet of the master, in a word, *studious* (or stoo-
djus) from which early American slang extracted the expression the
stooge, the eager-beaver assistant—academic or otherwise—who
does *anything* for favors from the master. The academic master,
meanwhile, the professor, publicly avows, declares, and professes
learning and inscribes it in works for the benefit of generations un-
born. Professionals of all stripes who deal with the infirm and the
aged often display their health and youth like a bustling cold front
that moves in and stiffens the landscape.

In fact, however, a reciprocity of giving and receiving is at work in
professional relationships that needs to be acknowledged. The student needs, to be sure, his teacher to assist him in learning, but so
also the professor needs his students. They provide him with regular
occasion and forum to work out what he has to say and to rediscover
his subject afresh through the discipline of sharing it with others. Patients need physicians, who loom larger in their lives than mates
during medical crises, but physicians also need patients. No one can
watch a doctor nervously approach retirement without realizing
how much he has needed his patients to be himself. Devout people

sometimes depend upon their ministers, but more than one young minister has ventured tentatively into the sickroom wondering what to say to a parishioner only to discover that the patient's composure ministers to his own faith.

In my day, a very popular book at divinity schools was Buber's *I and Thou*. The Jewish poet and theologian characterized the human bond as dialogical. Community is absent when conversation turns into monologue. Community requires addressing and being addressed, speaking and hearing, the tongue and the ear. Receiving is essential to community. It rescues love from the false posture of condescension and from a terrible isolation. A collection of givers alone can no more create a community than a stockpile of protons alone effects a chemical bond. It may be better to give than to receive, but it is more difficult to receive than to give. Community depends upon them both.

Love is the virtue that defines the role of giving in human life, but humility makes possible (and tolerable) the act of receiving. It keeps the self open to nourishment; it preserves the soul from hollowing out from within. Humility has a special place in self-recovery. It allows us to stay in touch with ourselves. What teacher stays alive as a teacher who does not remain a student? What preacher can preach the Word if he no longer hears it? What parent can comfort or discipline a child who does not recall the child in himself? Who can deal tenderly with the distress of the aged who cannot acknowledge his own distress before it?

The Ethics of the Aged

Perhaps we will take a first step toward re-entry into community with the aged when we are willing to take them seriously as moral beings. The worst kind of condescension toward any group is to deny them a moral significance, to refuse to subject their behavior to criticism, to pretend that they are moral nonentities, to treat them as toys. Ethicists unwittingly contribute to the exclusion of the elderly from the human race when they talk about the ethics of caretakers but neglect the ethics of care receivers.

Perhaps with full-span lives the norm, people may have to learn how to be aged as they once had to learn to be adult. It may soon be necessary and legitimate to criticise the long years of vapidity in which a healthy elderly person does little more than eat and play bingo, or who consumes excessive amounts of drugs, or who expects a self-indulgent stupidity to go unchecked. Just as the old should be convinced that whatever happens during senescence, they will never suffer exclusion, so they should understand that age does not exempt them from being despicable.[11]

A barely noticed but revolutionary moment occurs for a neglected group when its members are treated seriously as moral beings. As John Yoder has pointed out, the New Testament appears to be ethically conservative in its discussion of the duties of husbands and wives, parents and children, masters and slaves. It emphasizes the duties rather than the rights of the subordinates in each pair. In fact, the New Testament table of duties had a revolutionary potential in that it addressed *both* persons in the pair as moral agents. In this respect the New Testament writers broke with the Stoic tables of domestic duties, which addressed only the person in a superior position, as though only the more powerful had a moral existence. But in the New Testament "the *subordinate* person in the social order is *addressed as a moral agent.*"[12] There was no precedent for this in Hellenistic thought, argues Yoder. In addressing wives, children, and slaves, Christian Scripture assigned "*personal* moral responsibility to those who have no legal or moral status in their culture," making them decision makers. Western culture (and the church) have taken a long time catching up with this change of status. Not until the twentieth century did servants appear as more than comic figures in western drama. Until still more recently, blacks appeared only as comic figures, not to be taken seriously. But at least in principle the religious tradition itself provided for equal moral status.

Serious reflection on the moral status of the aged requires reflection on the specific virtues that age calls for. Such discussion will deteriorate into the sentimental if we do not remind ourselves that virtues hardly come automatically with age. Rather, they are structures of character that come with resolution, prayer, suffering, and persevering.

First on the list is *courage.* Westerners have too often restricted this virtue to the battlefield. But the soldier's prospect of death is uncertain, his separation from his loved ones temporary. Not so for the

aged, who face the finality of this separation and losses that are anything but temporary.

Caregivers need to evince the virtue of *humility.* Carereceivers need
the same virtue. The progressive loss of friends, job, bodily prowess,
and energy, the passing look on the face of the young that tells us we
are old—these experiences assault one's dignity; they humiliate. All
the care in the world will not avail to overcome the sting of humiliation; only humility can. It bears remembering that human, humility,
and earth itself—humus—have the same root. God took the dust of
the earth and breathed His spirit upon it and brought men and women
into being, human, humus, beset by humiliation but destined for
humility. Perhaps mid-life would not be so scary, so spoiled by preten-
sion, so shadowed by the fear of failure, if we knew how to keep our
feet in the soil of humility.

Patience is hardly a natural characteristic of old age. Advancing
age and infirmity provoke anger, frustration, and bitterness. Patience
is surely misunderstood when it is interpreted as a state of pure passivity. Patience is purposeful waiting, receiving, willing; it is a most
intense sort of activity; it is a way of taking control of one's spirit
precisely when all else goes out of control, when panic would send
one sprawling in all directions. Such patience is even more active
than that frenzied state of busy-ness that characterized mid-life.
Most of mid-life gets lived out in a state of passive activity. Despite
the appearance of great activity, our agendas are really set for us by
the drift of things, the volume of work to be done, the day's schedule
to keep up with. We tend to go on automatic pilot giving the illusion
of a great and heroic purposefulness. But sickness, sudden loss, protracted pain, the curtailed movement of old age, bring all this bustling to a halt and require us once again to get centered in the deepest
levels of our lives as purposeful beings.

The Benedictine monks used to talk about three other marks—
moral marks—of old age: *simplicitas, benignitas,* and *hilaritas.*[13]
Simplicity should mark the elderly, not merely because memory
lapses into its familiar repetitive grooves but because the pilgrim has
at long last learned how to travel light. *Benignity* is, according to the
monks, a kind of purified benevolence. It hardly goes with the terri-
tory of old age. Quite the contrary, the *ars moriendi* of the late Middle
Ages identified avarice as the chief besetting sin of the aged. The

closer one gets to the final dispossession of death, the more fiercely one may be inclined to clutch one's possessions: holding, grasping, managing, manipulating. Avarice has always been the sin of the hands. It strikes those for whom insecurity is maximal and mobility minimal, except for the reach of the hands. Benevolence opposes the tight-fistedness of avarice, not with the empty-handedness of death but with the open-handedness of love.

Hilarity is a curious virtue to associate with the aged. Are not the aged clinically given to more depression than their juniors? Anxiety over resources, grief over loss, insufficient exercise, broken sleep patterns, and diminished appetites precede and accompany depression. Yet the monks talk about *hilaritas*, a kind of celestial gaiety in those who have seen a lot, done a lot, grieved a lot, but now acquire that humored detachment of the fly on the ceiling looking down on the human scene.

Whatever special meaning hilarity may have had for the monk in the monastery, it is hardly reserved for the monks alone. Children are blessed if they happen to experience a lightness of spirit in their grandparents that offers sunny relief from their parents' gravity. In the year before his death Yeats expressed this hilarity in "Lapis Luzuli," a poem that spreads out the whole human scene of "old civilizations put to the sword" but closes by describing a Chinese carving in stone:

> Two Chinamen, behind them a third,
> Are carved in lapis lazuli,
> Over them flies a long legged bird,
> A symbol of longevity;
> The third, doubtless a serving man,
> Carries a musical instrument.
>
> Every discoloration of the stone,
> Every accidental crack or dent,
> Seems a water-course or an avalanche,
> Or lofty slope where it still snows
> Though doubtless plum or cherry branch
> Sweetens the little half-way house
> These Chinamen climb towards, and I
> Delight to imagine them seated there;
> There, on the mountain and the sky,

On all the tragic scene they stare,
One asks for mournful melodies;
Accomplished fingers begin to play.
Their eyes mid many wrinkles, their
eyes
Their ancient glittering eyes, are gay.[14]

Voluntary Communities and the Aged

The aged are agents as well as patients, but they still need care, and care requires the mobilization of social resources. Substantial government aid would, of course, be needed. But the demography of the aged makes it clear that we are headed for disaster if we handle their care solely in the conventional way in which we have tried to solve other problems. We have traditionally identified a special class of people as a "cause ," then appointed and paid a group of professionals to shield us from them by caring for them in our stead. In the discussion of philanthropy it was suggested that this strategy will not work because it is spiritually bankrupt. Economists point out that such a plan would also bankrupt us financially. The ratio of the middle-aged to the aged works against the scheme of freeing ourselves from the aged through money.

This raises the question, then, of other options. The major alternative to the huge bureaucracy that organizes professionals is the voluntary community that mobilizes amateurs. Chief among these are the synagogue and the church. De Tocqueville and other European observers have noted repeatedly the astonishing vitality of voluntary communities in America. Churches, synagogues, political parties, service organizations, parent-teacher associations, citizens' projects, and cause-oriented movements proliferate and abound. These voluntary communities constitute what Edmund Burke once called the "little platoons" in which people find community.

Voluntary communities, however, are in jeopardy today, partly because of the erosion of their financial support through inflation, but even more because of the erosion of their human support. They depend as much on the contributed time as on the treasure of their members. The church, foremost among them, has depended especially upon the volunteer time of women. The advent of the women's movement has altered dramatically the human resources available to the church and other voluntary communities. Women have moved increasingly into the professional world of work, into the mega-institutions, hierarchically organized, bureaucratically regularized, where they are increasingly better compensated but for jobs that are consuming and demanding. They have little time left for their families, much less for the voluntary communities that previously relied upon, to say nothing of exploited, them for services. The church as a traditional "outlet" for stymied women not only took advantage of their time and talent but annexed, through them, their husbands and children.

Justice forbids turning back the clock on the women's movement, but prudence requires thinking through the design of voluntary communities that can rely no longer on sexist patterns in the society at large for their support. This is a problem that churches share with other voluntary communities and that as an intellectual challenge, should enlist the interest of all those interested in the health of American society.

We may be moving into a period of history in which we need to sustain two kinds of social organizations: first, the traditional bureaucracies, the organizational equivalent of the Egyptian pyramids, massive, formal, geometrical, hierarchical; and second, small-scale, informal, and spontaneous communities that counterbalance the bureaucracies—just as the Egyptians once developed spontaneous, lyrical, naturalistic arts and crafts to compensate for the impersonal, massive, and impassible forms of the pyramid.

In such a dual world the church and other voluntary communities have several social functions. First, they must provide supplemental services beyond those that the bureaucracies provide. Bureaucracies are better at delivering technical services than at responding to personal needs. Amateurs who offer companionship and friendship to the elderly sometimes may address their deeper needs better than those who offer expertise. Second, bureaucracies need the critical check of outside representatives on their boards of directors and amateurs who frequent the halls of their institutions to stand as advocate and shelter for those who need an intermediary between themselves and professionals. This is not to propose an adversarial relationship between amateurs and professionals. But only too often professional teachers, nurses, or health-care practitioners develop a defensive, proprietary attitude toward institutions for which they are responsible. The sheer repetitiveness of their contact with the distressed tends to give them spiritual callousness. The amateur who darts in and out of the institution has no right to feel morally superior to them. But, at the same time, the amateur has the advantage of seeing the environment with the eyes of the inexperienced stranger. Every institution needs to be exposed to the "dumb" question: Why do you do this rather than that? Why this kind of building, not that? One needs to sort out the differences between procedures that merely serve the convenience of institutions and their managers and those that best serve the inmates' needs.

Further, outsiders can bridge the gap between institution and community, making needs known. Otherwise, institutions that idealists originally founded will deteriorate eventually into custodial bins. Historian David Rothman has noted a pattern of decline and fall across the decades in our total institutions—prisons, hospitals, mental hospitals, asylums, and, he could have added, nursing homes. Amateurs alone cannot run our institutions; their work can be too inept, too easily discouraged, too episodic, to dispense with the professional. Nevertheless, we must find ways of bringing the outside community into contact with the service bureaucracies if the latter are not to founder.

Finally, voluntary communities will need not only to supplement, criticize, and support the institutions already in place but also to experiment with alternative patterns for the delivery of care. In one church basement in San Francisco, elderly folk were receiving meals. The church and other cooperating institutions provided this service through a federal grant. At first glance the basement setting was conventional enough. The elderly ate. But then it became clear that retarded and variously handicapped folk served the meal. It took the federal government to support the program, but it took the church to conceive it, a cooperative venture between the two. With one stroke the program benefits not only the elderly but also another deprived group and finally a middle-class community of organizers and hosts.

Bold experiments will be required against the day that the great institutions and skyscrapers about us, which look so formidable and permanent, should crack and decay. However, the voluntary communities may not be able to devise attractive alternatives unless in the course of their philanthropies they also recognize themselves to

be beneficiaries at the hands of those whom they serve—and recover
their lost human power of *veneration.*

NOTES

1. Alvin Rabushka and Bruce Jacobs, "Are Old Folks Really Poor?
Herewith a View at Some Common Views," *New York Times*, Feb. 15, 1980.

2. Ronald Blythe, *The View in Winter* (N.Y.: Harcourt Brace Jovanovich,
1979), p. 73.

3. Philip Slater, *The Pursuit of Loneliness: American Culture at the
Breaking Point* (Boston: Beacon Press, 1976).

4. For a detailed treatment of total institutions and the impulse to sequester, see William F. May, "Institutions as Symbols of Death," *Journal of the
American Academy of Religion* 44 (June, 1976): 212-23.

5. Michael Foucault, *Madness and Civilization: A History of Insanity in
the Age of Reason* (New York: Random House, 1973).

6. Blythe, *View in Winter*, p. 88.

7. Ibid., p. 82.

8. Ibid., p. 119.

9. Ibid., p. 104.

10. I associate this ethic with Protestants more than with Catholics or
Jews because the latter two groups have generally had, as immigrants, a
more powerful sense of common bond with those whom they have helped.

11. Blythe, *View in Winter*, pp. 22-23.

12. John Yoder, *The Politics of Jesus* (Grand Rapids, Mich.: Wm. B.
Eerdmans, 1972), p. 1974.

13. For a study of the Benedictines, see Blythe's chapter on the "Prayer
Route."

14. William Butler Yeats, "Lapis Lazuli," in *The Collected Poems of W. B.
Yeats*, definitive edition (New York: Macmillan, 1956), pp. 291-93.

A popular TV commercial promises that "if you've got your health, you've got everything." What is meant by "health"? Is it indeed that human possession second to none among a great number of goods? On the contrary: health is not a possession won by increasing consumption of elixirs, pills, and health services. Rather, it is a state of being achieved when a person severs his dependency upon the production and consumption of commodities and recovers his power of subsistence—"the ability and freedom to grow one's own food, construct one's own shelter, (and) move oneself spatially and spiritually." A healthy person thus is one whose powers for self-reliance have been activated.

SUBSISTENCE Ivan Illich

The term "health" may be used in somewhat the same way we use the terms "freedom" or "dignity", "privacy" or "justice." To speak about a healthy society should not be less meaningful than to speak about one that is free or just. And to say that a society is free, or that it fosters health, or protects privacy, is to say something about what that society's people believe, how they act, how they *are*. Such assertions say something about the shape, the *Gestalt* of a society.

Specifically, health may be discussed as a characteristic of industrial societies and their possible successors. Now health, like freedom, can be attributed to pre-industrial and traditional extra-European societies. In a metaphorical sense, or with careful qualifications, that which our kind of society means by the words "health" or "education" or "transportation" can be predicated of Babylonians or the Chol. Our concern is not with these, however, but with health as it exists in societies which use explicit and rational means to give form to their care of health. It is not only the shape of society's health, but also the process which leads to that shape, which is crucial. The public pursuit of health in a modern society can be viewed as articulating a set of political, social, technical, or cultural issues.

The health to which public decisions give a shape, specific to each society, is something other than one individual's personal well-

45

being. It is also something other than medicine, be it preventative, curative, social, or ecological. It means the social framework for a people's aliveness, together with the support for this structuring. This kind of health cannot be fully measured quantitatively. All its aspects which can be counted, taken together, comprise only one plane in a multidimensional topography of health. Indicators such as infant survival, the incidence of specific disease, cure rates, access to therapy, and accident prevention are, by themselves, as meaningless as the number of passenger miles and their distribution when taken as indicators of mutual access within a society. We must also use ethical and esthetic criteria to evaluate the freedom or health of a society, to compare it with others and to compare it with its own past and possible future. To speak about the structure of health in a society means to examine that society's vitality, the aliveness of its members in relation to one another: that is, to speak about the whole of society from a particular perspective, namely, the extent to which a subsistence mode of life characterizes individual and social action.

To a great extent the public decisions that give shape to a society's health fall into three areas: (1) those that determine the balance of privileges among different groups and classes of people; (2) those that deal with the creation, limits, and use of technical means; and (3) those that regulate the society's tolerance of distinct lifestyles of different kinds of people. These three distinct vectors of option determine the shape of health in modern society.

Only ten years ago the description of health in industrial societies as a Gestalt of aliveness would have been difficult to imagine. During the sixties the myth of health production had not yet been formally challenged. Further, the contribution of subsistence activities to industrial economics still lay in the blind spot of economic and social analysis. Belief in what I call the myth of health production now appears naive, even more dubious than the general modern myth which holds that mankind is destined to live by the product of its wage labor. A discussion of health from the perspective of demedicalization can, therefore, serve to dispel the more pervasive illusion about the economic nature of human wants and needs.

In highly industrialized societies just ten years ago health care primarily meant access to the doctor or, in the case of disease, to insurance payments. People in general, together with most contributors to the public discussion, seemed unaware of the degree to which the perception of disease, prevention, cure, and impairment had been radically altered during just a few decades. These perceptions had been narrowed down to the needs for which physicians could provide services. Health had been medicalized in view of the clinic.

During the seventies health ceased to be measured primarily in view of the number of hospital beds, specialists, and insurance coverage available per million inhabitants. Public discussion replaced a clinically medicalized view of health by three distinct but sometimes overlapping issues: (1) sickness prevention, from seat belts to the control of additives; (2) health instruction, in order to standardize people's hygienic behavior; and (3) training in and supervision of self-care, in order to make everyone into a doctor's assistant. These ideas became characteristic of the trans-clinical medicalization of health during the seventies. Meanwhile, high costs, leading to the rationing of therapeutic health care, epidemiological evidence on the relative inefficiency of health services, and the egalitarian commitments of the welfare state all supported the emphasis on professional programs in the areas of social medicine, hygiene, and self-care.

Although we witnessed a major shift from the physician to the health planner and educator during the seventies, a further increase in the medicalization of health occurred. Although the public authorities in some countries succeeded in putting brakes on the runaway budgets of hospital-based medicine, the overall total of programs designed to foster health increased through ecological, educational, and urbanistic programs of legislatures and bureaucracies. The major policies in the shaping of the society's health remained the same: how to produce health care, how to organize its consumption, and how to make other forms of production and consumption less damaging to human beings and less destructive of the environment. The transition from "health care production and delivery" (an expression, now rightly ridiculed, but still used with impunity in American medical schools in 1975) to interest in a rational development of consumer society does mean progress, albeit progress in the medicalization of health.

This medicalization of health is thoroughly consistent with the view of man's nature that still dominates the most widely opposed ideologies and positions in the world's political arena. According to this view, mankind has developed by historical necessity to the stage where basic needs must now be supplied through the processes of industrial production. Mankind, this vision claims, is made up of possessive individuals who live in an environment where values are scarce by their very nature, and who make each of their decisions in light of some marginal utility. In the service of people thus imagined, science and technology are useful if they can be applied to the industrial process of production in order to increase outputs, therby either satisfying new needs or relieving scarcity in the satisfaction of basic needs.

Once man is conceived as industrial producer of consumer goods, satisfaction is inevitably scarce—where one gains, another loses. Public life becomes concerned mainly with the increase of production and the ordering of distribution. Politics, in this view of reality, is guided by economics, the science dealing with scarce values. For *homo economicus*, life is reduced to production and consumption, the former typified by the male dressed for work, the latter by the housewife surrounded by gadgets, each active in the production and reproduction, respectively, of the political economy. No wonder that in such a society increased production and reproduction together seem the very image and symbol of health.

This notion of man as producer and consumer is now being challenged. Exacting research and experiments in self-reliance converge to question the ideal of employed males, married to housekeepers who also seek outside jobs, both aided by doctor, teacher, and other professionals to reproduce their like. A disinterested study of philosophy, ideology, and culture clearly reveals how completely incompatible our most entrenched ideas are with the reality perceived by other ages and societies. The deeply satisfying and successful experience of modern subsistence farmers, together with those who approximate such a mode of life, plainly show how absurd it is to claim that the alienation represented by one or more generations of consumerdom means an irreplaceable loss of competence in activities necessary for independent living. But another result of contemporary thought and practice is even more important for this argument. For the first time in a century social analysis is taking account of subsistence activities which, it is recognized, must continue even in the most highly developed industrial societies. We now know that nowhere except in industrial societies does man depend upon commodities for most of his satisfactions or needs. We also know that even in industrial societies, man does not live off consumption alone. But acknowledgment and discussion of this latter fact have been so thoroughly tabooed that academicians and politicians today can suddenly achieve recognition and fame announcing its "discovery."

People integrated into industrial societies have radically different needs from those of people anywhere else. Their needs are defined for them by goods and services provided by experts, not by things and actions they can make or do themselves. Such needs have been called "commodity-intensive," needs for products resulting from a production process that fuses labor and capital. Social and economic progress, growth, and development are simply different terms to designate the replacement of subsistence activities by commodities, the substitution of competence in caring for oneself by discipline in production and consumption, the displacement of variety by standard brands and uniformity.

Modern language as used to describe the human predicament, particularly when designating those perceived by the speaker as "poor," had been profoundly shaped by the view of economic man. Not only the disciples of Marx but also those of Freud speak about the "production" of love, ideas, and sentiments, and even of society itself. Through this misuse of language the distinction between subsistence activity and economic performance has been veiled. Yet only people whose income depends on the reproduction of "care" will dare to equate the service they provide with love, or the "correct" language they teach with vernacular speech. The use of the term "production," when speaking about subsistence activities, is the best way to confuse this issue and to blind oneself to the existence of a wide range of subsistence activities, even in commodity-intensive life settings. Even under intensive care, people can be said to stay alive only insofar as they shape their own thoughts, sentiments, and actions in spite of the service they consume. The importance of subsistence activities for the very existence of political and economic society is one of the major insights of research during the last few years. The inapplicability of concepts taken from formal economic theory to describe and analyze these activities is a corollary. This insight may prove to be the single most important source of social innovation in the early eighties.

Therefore, one can maintain that even in the most highly developed modern society two distinct domains are complementary and in synergy to create the values which make life possible and desirable: the area of subsistence and that of formal economic activities—the dimension that personal aliveness contributes to social reality, and that which can or must be produced. Perhaps most people, when they speak about the health of a society, mean the degree and shape of subsistence. Defined in this way, health will be high when survival in a society depends principally upon subsistence activities. Health will be low when subsistence activities have been largely replaced by the production and consumption of commodities. It will be high where the ability to initiate and participate in subsistence activities is well distributed throughout the society, low where this freedom is available only to the few—either as a hobby of the privileged or as a necessity of the marginal. Health will be high where social structure, law, and technique make survival through one's own direct action possible and varied, and low where people are deprived of such conditions and tools. Subsistence means the ability and freedom to grow one's own food, construct one's own shelter, move oneself spatially and spiritually. People achieving subsistence ask whether institutional assistance is more than bureaucratic interference, whether clinical checkups do more than create dependence, whether instruction effects more than numbness. The shape of health in a society means essentially the intensity and style of subsistence. The shape of health in a modern society means especially that domain of subsistence which continues to exist despite widespread commodity intensity, surviving even where both paid and unpaid jobs are increasingly dominated by the commodities of industrial production.

If health is the shape that subsistence activities take in a modern society, then the striving for health is mostly a struggle for conditions under which self-reliance or autonomous activities can flourish. These efforts do not supersede or invalidate class conflict; rather, they give it new meaning. In the hypothesis that man is understood primarily as producer of basic satisfactions—a view common to Marx, Adam Smith, and Milton Friedman—the struggle for outputs, for commododities, comes first. Not so in working for a healthy society. Here, protection of the domain of subsistence against compulsory consumption assumes public priority in the several actions through which people give shape to their society. The first task in a struggle for the highest possible intensity of autonomy, that is, of health, is the reordering of the relative status of production and subsistence. In industrial society the production of goods and services is the central concern—subsistence activities are viewed as vestiges not yet completely replaced. But even with escalators and elevators, people in Manhattan still climb stairs, especially if they are poor. Even with costly emergency services, some babies are born outside of hospitals. In spite of pre-kindergarten instruction, children still learn walking and talking from persons not paid to appear and speak correctly. Despite great economic growth, subsistence still survives. Industrial society today, then, restricts health to the shape of a discriminated, marginal aspect of life for most people. In a healthy society, on the contrary, subsistence is pivotal. That is, the innate ability of people to cope directly with reality, relying to the greatest practicable extent on their own resources, is of fundamental significance for the society. And what term is more proper than "health" to designate the ability to cope with pleasure and pain in a creative manner? The legal protection of the *freedom to live by doing* is thus the principal issue in any politics of health.

The end of the seventies was distinguished from earlier periods of social criticism by a multiplicity of actions and movements in which people defended their right to spaces of freedom from consumption. The phrase "to unplug a neighborhood from commodity circuits" was invented in Chicago. Bourgeois society has greatly treasured freedom of expression. But up until now this has been interpreted mainly as a freedom of thought and word. The new movements insist on the freedom of practical, *living* expression. People demand their right to withdraw from both production and consumption, and to do so for a large part of their lives. They claim their right to an environment of relative poverty where they can fare basically on what they do. They reverse the prevalent relationship between production and subsistence, desiring the least possible production necessary for a comfortable and independent life. And they know that survival and, therefore, health, cannot be achieved or regulated by decree. Thus they seek the necessary tolerance and protection of the deviance they generate through their style of health.

Giving priority to the social and legal protection of innumerable different styles of self-reliance against the dictatorship of a productivist society does not supplant the struggle for equality—this problem is simply redefined. If issues that pit subsistence against compulsory consumption are placed on a vertical axis, then the equal right to distinct styles of subsistence would fall on a horizontal axis. While an independent mode of living will take the form of a legal claim to the protection of freedom for various lifestyles, the struggle for access to equal resources to maintain such lifestyles can best be envisaged as a renewed form of political action. Access to commodities which cannot be produced in the local community is an issue that can be voted on by common representatives of groups choosing many different lifestyles, analogous to the way in which Christians and Jews, Puerto Ricans and WASPS can work together in the Liberal party of New York.

But the right to live one's own form of self-determination, and the equal right to an equitable share in basic resources—air, land, water—are not the only key issues that determine the shape of health in contemporary society. Another is public control over the technical means by which resources are developed. The right to a specific way of living is of immediate concern to those who have chosen it; this is a question of freedom. But the distribution of scarce resources is a zero-sum game, where someone loses when another gains. The elimination of atomic generators, of capital punishment, of artificial mutants from society's tool kit is a universal affair. This is true both because it is a decision which limits the zero-sum game in which the scarce resources under political dispute are produced, and because it defends, at this cost, a characteristic of the environment that is equally significant for all, no matter what lifestyle they have chosen.

Health, then, can be defined as the manifold shape that subsistence activities take in a society. This shape is achieved through decisions in which the society's members participate, and which determine for the society at a given moment three parameters: the degree of freedom with which subsistence can be pursued, the degree of equity with which resources for this pursuit are accessible, and the degree to which the society's environment is effectively protected.

In this view of the world, access to medical care in all its specialized professional forms is reduced to one of the many resources that some communites only may be interested in claiming and financing.

*Feelings—"our subjective awareness of our own emotional state"—
mark us as creatures alive to our own powers, or weaknesses. Feelings enable us to confront, judge, and transcend the limitations of
our human state. Feelings "are the fine instruments that shape decision making in an animal cursed and blessed with intelligence and
freedom." Feelings, positively and creatively harnessed, sharpen the
moral sense, developing that awareness of the right and the good
which enables us to act rationally, justly, and virtuously.*

FEELINGS

Willard Gaylin

There is an incredible amount of confusion about feelings and emotions in both the minds of the public and the attention of the "experts." Even the nomenclature presents a problem. Generally speaking, the field of psychology has settled down to the use of three
terms: "emotion" is the general term which encompasses the feeling
tone, the biophysiological state, and even the chemical changes that
we are beginning to understand underlie the sensations we experience. "Affect," introduced from psychoanalysis, is used to describe
the dominant emotional tone of an individual and is particularly
used in relationship to our recognition of the feelings of others.
"Feeling" is our subjective awareness of our own emotional state. It
is that which we experience, that which we know about our current
emotional condition.

Given the central importance of feelings in our everyday life, one
would think that the psychological and psychoanalytical literature
would be dominated by them. It is not so. Perhaps it is unsettling in a
scientific and logical age to place much value on such a subjective,
unmeasureable—such an "irresponsible"—subject as feelings. Perhaps feelings are too close to our vulnerable central core to allow for
comfortable evaluation. Perhaps it is simple that in a technological
society, which values the measurable, the visible, the palpable, and
the objectifiable, feelings embarrass us by defying our most respected tools of investigation.

Obviously, different cultures, and the individuals within them, vary in their attitudes about feelings. What is emotionally acceptable in the streets of Palermo would seem aberrant in the cool reserve of Stockholm. There is significant difference even in more similar cultures, such as Germany and England, as Naomi Bliven comments: "My reading has given me the impression that Germans have been more tolerant than English-speakers of men who throw tantrums, get into flaps, and publicly exhibit wide swings of emotion." She then compares the acceptance of Wilhelm II by German people with English attitudes, and notes that

> Wilhelm II was always giving offense in England, though his own subjects seem not to have found him unstable or even notably unattractive. It is difficult to imagine someone as lacking in self-control and good manners as Ludendorff achieving high command in an English-speaking army—the English used to send gifted but temperamental military men, like Gordon and Wingate, to places like the Sudan and Burma, the boondocks of empire.[1]

She is particularly horrified that the Germans were said to have found Hitler charming. Here she is, of course, referring not to the monstrous political actions of Hitler, toward which the word "charm" is almost obscenely juxtaposed, but to his public personality. She is incredulous that the Germans "found charm in a man who gobbled sweets, made disgusting comments on food at the table, engaged in staring matches, bragged about his intelligence, and flew into a rage when anybody questioned one of his statements." She wisely recognizes that cultural attitudes about the display of public emotion are permitted to vary when she concludes: "Perhaps it is a matter of other places, other mores." While we may differ in our cultural attitudes toward display of emotion, no culture can afford to disparage the importance of feelings.

Feeling is—if not all—almost all. It serves utility and sensuality. Feelings are the fine instruments that shape decision making in an animal cursed and blessed with intelligence, and the freedom which is its corollary. They are signals directing us toward goodness, safety, pleasure, and group survival. Feelings can, like every other aspect of our humanity, be corrupted from their original purposes. As hunger drove primitive man to the nurture required for life, gluttony can drive modern man to the obesity that destroys. So, too, with feelings. Jealousy, which serves the struggle for survival, can deteriorate into envy, which draws defeat even from victory. We can be overwhelmed by inappropriate guilt, anxiety, or shame. Mental illness is usually a mere disarray of the ingredients of survival. All that is necessary is rearrangement. Feelings are internal directives essential for human life. In addition, and not just in passing, they are their own rewards. They are the means and the ends. All goodness and pleasure must be ultimately perceived in the realm of feelings. It is in the balance of small passions of daily existence that we measure and value our lives.

Yet the public at large is confused about the meaning of feelings and the propriety of their public expression. The confusion is exploited by the continuing flow of "how to" books that guide the perplexed and despairing to inner peace via conflicting and contradictory pathways. On the one hand, there is the "emotions are bad" school, which sees them as stormy intruders on the tranquil sea of life. Here shame and guilt are most frequently denounced as unnecessary and "neurotic." But shame and guilt are noble emotions essential in the maintenance of civilized society and vital for the development of some of the most refined and elegant qualities of human potential—generosity, service, self-sacrifice, unselfishness, and duty.

Then there is the theory that accepts emotions as perfectly permissible signs of the healthy body's response to distress, provided these emotions are not contained. In this school of thought emotions are obliged to be discharged into the environment. This is the "emotions as pus" concept. You must bring your anger to a head; if you cannot, the good doctor will lance the boil and discharge the venom. What must be expressed is almost always anger—occasionally, anxiety. It is a principle that has found particular favor in a time and a subculture that have glorified self-expression. Its credo is captured by the vulgar but descriptive expression "Let it all hang out." I have never felt that people's inner feelings have some claim to public recognition. Quite the contrary; for the most part, the private life of the narcissist, like the private parts of the exhibitionist, ought not be hung out—uninvited—in the public space.

Even if one does accept the concept that the discharged emotion has a particular moral standing, how does one move from this assumption to the next, that self-improvement can be achieved by generating the emotion so that it may later be relieved? In other words, if one accepts the fact that fevers are bad and ought to be reduced by dissipating the heat into the environment through cold-water immersion, alcohol rubs, or aspirin, this hardly means that there is something therapeutic in generating a fever in the first place simply so that dissipation can occur. The problem with people who have pent-up emotions is usually not their inability to express them but their incredible capacity to generate them. They do not need a weekend marathon of provocation and humiliation to express the very emotions that they generate to excess *without* provocation.

Obviously, the cathartic, howling, and confrontation theories arise from a sloppy reading of early Freud. In his first speculations in the *Studies in Hysteria* (1893), Freud postulated with his colleague Breuer that neurosis was due to the accidental encapsulation of emotion that failed to be discharged. Even in that first treatise he was not so naive as to assume that the simple discharge of the emotion by whatever means would alleviate the condition. At any rate, Freud spent the next fifty years of his life modifying that position, recognizing its oversimplification, and building the theory of psychoanalysis that saw behavior as purposive, dynamic, defensive, and meaningful. He grew to see the accidental encapsulation of emotion, like a foreign body, as a grossly oversimplified concept of the etiology of neurosis.

In the twentieth century there gradually emerged a general theory of behavior that progressively reinforced the sense of the "wisdom of the body." More and more it became apparent that behavior was purposeful and goal-directed. Even seemingly "foolish" or discomforting behavioral symptons that were originally viewed *as* the disease were proved to be defenses *against* the disease. Fever is not a sickness but the body's adaptive mechanism to increase the rate of biochemical defenses by increasing the temperature. Similarly, phobias, obsessions, and delusions are attempts to control, limit, and cope with unbearable emotional states.

Obviously, specific feelings serve multiple and varied purposes, depending on the nature of the feelings. But more important is the recognition that emotions are useful and serve adaptive purposes.

Why do people have emotions and feelings? What good are they? Perhaps here an analogy is useful. We know by the nature of their crude systems that certain lower forms of life cannot experience emotions. They have no brain or central nervous system. They do, however, have a built-in stimulus/response mechanism, so that when something noxious is touched, an innate and automatic withdrawal mechanism occurs. An emotion therefore is not essential to trigger a protective maneuver. Even when the subjective feeling of pain is present, it need not be the initiator of the response. In simple situations the response is simultaneous with the feeling or may even precede it. If pain is severe enough, a momentary sense of shock occurs and the pain is not experienced until well after the contact. So if you put your finger to a hot plate, the withdrawal is likely to occur well before the pain is experienced. When the trauma is sufficient, there is often a surprising absence of pain for a few seconds until the overwhelming flood of painful experience occurs.

What is the purpose of that subjective sense of pain—the feeling, if you will? It is a message to the cognitive processes, to the thinking brain, and to our intelligence, which is so often wrongfully seen as the opposite of emotion. It is a signal of danger whose purpose is to direct behavior. It is part of the learning experience. While in the extreme case cited the experience of pain is not needed to effect the protective maneuver, it still serves a purpose. It is stored in memory and in other cases where there are choices, it will be recalled, thus becoming a guide in determining future behavior.

Feelings, therefore, particularly the complex and subtle range of feelings in human beings, testify to our capacity for choice and learning. Feelings are the instruments of rationality, not—as some would have it—alternatives to it. Because we are intelligent creatures— meaning that we are freed from instinctive and patterned behavior to a degree unparalleled in the animal kingdom—we are capable of ,and dependent upon, the use of rational choice to decide our futures. Feelings become guides to that choice. We are not just passive responders, as some lower life forms are, to that which the environment offers us. We can avoid certain conditions, select others, and anticipate both, and, moreover—via anticipation—we can even modify the nature of the environment. Feelings, then, are fine tunings directing the ways in which we will meet and manipulate our environment.

Feelings of anxiety, boredom, tension, and agitation alert us to the sense of something wrong; more important, by the subtle distinctions of their messages they indicate something of the nature of the impending danger and direct us to specific kinds of adaptive maneuvers to avoid, prevent, or change the incipient threat. Feelings of guilt allow us to model our behavior against certain ideals and register the point at which we have moved away from those ideals or have not yet acheived them. Equally important, because of the pain of the emotion, it will—like a thermostatic control—initiate the very process of moving us back closer to the nature of our ideal.

Of course, emotions and feelings can go out of balance. It is the nature of an animal endowed with free will to design his own future, at least in part. But that freedom allows us to design badly—i.e., maladaptively—or to design well.

There is also an expressive side to emotions, and while not primarily dealing with that aspect—the part of emotion that is visualized by others—it is important here to see that, like feeling, it also serves a purpose. The affects, in allowing others to view our emotional state, transfer one individual's experience to the group at large and by so doing enhance group survival.

The contagious nature of emotion is essential to a group animal like *Homo sapiens*; it allows us, with our feelings, to forewarn those around us. Each individual becomes an extension of the group, serving the mutual needs of the whole. If one lone "scout" perceives a danger, his very emotion advertises the fact. Words are not necessary. Affects are simple alternatives to the spoken word and as such are the "language" of most herding animals. When one member perceives that which the group has yet to perceive, it serves as an early-warning system.

While we are not technically herd animals like cattle or sheep, we are also not isolates. We must live in groups; other people are like nutrients for us and are absolutely essential for our survival. Certain feelings like shame force us to forgo selfish pleasures for the benefit of the group at large. They indicate our unwitting sense that all individual survival is dependent on, and therefore must defer to, group survival. Even without knowing why, we respond to the feelings of others. Emotions are contagious. Anxiety moves like a ripple through a crowd. Tears evoke tears, even when the content or cause of the original distress is unknown.

Emotions, then, are not just directives to ourselves but directives from others to us, indicating that we have been seen, that we have been understood, that we have been appreciated, that we have made contact. Unfortunately, we are confused about the very purpose and value of emotion. We have gotten into the bind of not being sure whether the healthy person is emotion-free, emotionally open, a person with minimal emotion, or a person with certain select emotions. We are often ashamed of the wrong emotions. In our concern for power and assertion, we overvalue rage and demean guilt.

Feelings are difficult, nonpalpable, slippery things even by definition. In that sense they are immune to the kind of analysis to which most behavior is typically exposed. They are difficult to quantify, communicate, even to distinguish within ourselves one from the other. With feelings, there is also a sloppiness in public usage that follows closely on the difficulty of definition. People know how they feel and therefore assume that others feel the same. Communication, they assume, need only be suggested, so the language of feelings is imprecise to the point of making generalization hazardous.

In order to overcome this imprecision, we resort to drawing on shared experience, thus avoiding the labeling process altogether. People use the expression "You know how you feel when. . . ." But it is intriguing to find out how often people do *not* agree "how they feel when," and how they even confuse and misunderstand the nature of the emotion they may be experiencing.

The degree of misunderstanding tends to vary with the emotion. Most people recognize fear. On the other hand, people often seem visibly and obviously angry and yet have no genuine awareness that they are angry; or, worse, they misinterpret their anger for another emotion. It is not uncommon to hear a clearly angry patient talk about feeling "agitated" or "anxious." One patient when angry felt a unique kind of internal "pressure" of the most unpleasant sort, which he assumed to be some sort of abdominal spasm. He could not "honestly say that it was painful," but "gnawing, unpleasant" were close. "Something akin to hunger," he once said. This was as near to acknowledging the emotional state that this reserved man could allow. In time it became clear that this emotion, perceived as a physiological and physical phenomenon, was indeed an anger that he somehow denied entrance into his world of recognition.

When we leave the basic and primitive emotions and enter into the range of more subtle, more specifically and exclusively human emotions of shame, embarrassment, guilt, pride, and so forth, we find how confused people are in the labeling of even their own feelings.

In one of the recent books supplying prescriptions for happiness, a chapter heading reads: "The Useless Emotions—Guilt and Worry." Since worry here is used to mean all anxiety, the author has managed with this title to dismiss the basic props for individual survival and group responsibility.

Guilt is not only a uniquely human experience; its cultivation in people—along with shame—serves the noblest, most generous and humane character traits that distinguish our species. We can assume that everyone has felt anxiety; with guilt we are in a different situation. First, some people have never experienced the feeling of guilt. They are not, however, the lucky ones, nor are we fortunate in having them in our midst. The failure to feel guilt is the basic flaw of the psychopath, or antisocial person, who is capable of committing crimes of the vilest sort without remorse or contrition.

Another difficulty in writing about guilt is that even those who have experienced the feeling do not readily distinguish it from such differing emotions as fear and anger. In addition, it is confused with certain similar emotions (shame and guilty fear), so that people are never quite sure—in feeling as well as usage—whether they are experiencing guilt or the related emotions. Again, a rush to the dictionary is no help. Quite to the contrary, it may confound. It was with some chagrin that, after having already completed a paper on conscience in which I talked about the feeling of guilt, I discovered that the most intimidating and authoritative of lexicons, the Oxford English Dictionary, does not allow that guilt *is* an emotion. I was chastened by the OED, which in its usual generous way acknowledged dozens of definitions of guilt, none of which included the emotional state. It sees guilt exclusively as an act or state of wrongdoing: a failure, offense, crime, delinquency, or culpability, but not an emotion! It specifically cautions against "misuse for 'sense of guilt.'" As is its wont, it then cites for eternal shame down through the centuries a Reverend Mr. Tillotson, who committed the error of confusing the state of guilt with the sense of guilt, i.e., the feeling. In this case I stand with Mr. Tillotson rather than the OED, and I will accept his definition of guilt as "nothing else but trouble arising in our mind from our consciousness of having done contrary to what we are verily persuaded was our Duty."

What, then, is the feeling of guilt? More often than not, it is confused with two other closely related emotions. One is shame and the second is something that is best called "guilty fear." If you were to ask a typical group of people to define a situation in which they recently felt guilty, it is possible that at least half would describe not guilt but rather guilty fear. I have tried this experiment in classrooms and social situations and the results were always the same. Some of the answers that indicate guilty fear are the "I was caught in the act of" category. A larger percentage might be classified as the "I was about to be caught." Everyone knows that panicky feeling when we are in the process of an immoral, illegal, or disapproved action, and we feel the hot breath of authority down our necks. When we assume that we will be imminently apprehended, we have this rush of sickening feeling which is not guilt but guilty fear. The primary emotion is fear. It is *guilty* fear because it is fear that is clearly related to some wrongdoing we acknowledge. If you are casually driving at sixty-five miles per hour (when you know that fifty-five is the legal limit) and suddenly hear the sound of a siren as you catch a glimpse of the highway patrol in your rear-view mirror, that slightly nauseating rush of feeling through your chest is guilty fear. It is fear you are experiencing.

Here "guilt" is only the modifier, the adjective to describe the kind of fear that is felt. If we can experience unjustified fear and irrational fear, we are also free to feel fear which we know stems from our having done something that will elicit punishment. The emotion is related not to the act of having been bad but to the fear of getting what we deserve for it, or to the fear of getting caught.

To return to that scene on the highway: as you apprehensively watch the approaching police car, you are amazed to find that he passes you by to flag down the Porsche which whizzed past you only moments before. What do you feel? If it is relief, then the emotion experienced with the first sound of the siren was guilty fear. If there are a few strange ones among you who are disappointed, then I grant you felt true guilt.

The distinguishing test between the two is in its relation to exposure and apprehension. When guilty fear alone is present, getting away with it—the avoidance of punishment—brings immediate relief and delight. Guilt, however, wants exposure; it needs expiation and forgiveness.

Maxine Kingston, in her memoir, describes guilt as an unbearably constrictive feeling in her throat. (I myself always experience guilt as a nauseating feeling somewhere between the upper chest, reserved for fear, and the abdomen.) The only relief for this feeling is to confront the individual who is both responsible for the feeling and capable of relieving it—to the child, almost invariably the parent:

> . . . I had grown inside me a list of over two hundred things that I had to tell my mother so that she would know the true things about me and stop the pain in my throat. When I first started counting, I had only thirty-six items. . . . If only I could let my mother know the list, she—and the world—would become more like me, and I would never be alone again. I would pick a time of day when my mother was alone and tell her one item a day; I'd be finished in less than a year. If the telling got excruciating and her anger too bad, I'd tell five items once a week like the Catholic girls; and I'd still be through in a year, maybe ten months. . . . I had decided to start with the earliest item—when I had smashed a spider against the white side of the house; it was the first thing I killed. I said, clearly, "I killed a spider," and it was nothing; she did not hit me or throw hot starch at me. It sounded like nothing to me too. . . . Relieved because she said nothing but only continued squeezing the starch, I went away feeling pretty good. Just two hundred and six more items to go.[2]

I first realized the oppositional nature of guilty fear to guilt in one of the most vivid memories of early life, involving what I then considered a revelation. Being the eldest of three boys, I was often left "in charge" for small periods of time. Even when not in charge, I would assume authority or privilege. Obviously, as the eldest I possessed a whole repertoire of tormenting and manipulative devices, and characteristically the only retaliative device of merit left to the younger ones was, "I'm going to tell Daddy on you." I remember now with a chilling awareness—although the nature of the heinous

crimes I had committed has long since been comfortably forgotten—
a moment when my younger brother said precisely that over something evil enough to ensure wrath and punishment. I had that sick,
rushing, chesty feeling which is the mark of guilty fear. At that moment I experienced one of the few (if not the only) epiphanies in my
personal life. He is going to tell Daddy I did that, I thought. But
Daddy is not here. I can tell Daddy that I did *not* do it. It had never
occurred to me before that reality could be modified, that indeed the
past only existed in the relating of it. I had discovered lying! I had
such a sense of power, joy, and delight that its parallel in life is hard
to recall. A powerful new tool had been handed to me. It filled me
with an indescribable sense of pleasure and freedom.

Only later in life would I experience true guilt and it surely is not
coincidence that it was also in relation to lying; to this day there is
nothing that can invoke true guilt more readily in me than telling a
lie, even a white lie. One of my first memories of the torture of guilt
was when I had lied to that same father, whom I adored and to whom
lying was anathema. The Saturday afternoon movies were a tradition
for the prepubescents in our neighborhood. Everybody went, and always to the local neighborhood movie (no "big" streets to cross). I
had left my sweater at the movies—a reversible tragedy—but somehow when I was asked where my sweater was, I said, "Grandma's."
Surely I was old enough to realize that the lie would be exposed. This
doting grandmother, after all, was acquainted with my father. It was
a gratuitous lie, bound to be detected, and about something which
could not have concerned my father less. The longest day of my
young life was waiting for him to come home so that I could blurt
out my confession.

Guilty fear is relieved when the threat of punishment disappears.
True guilt seeks, indeed embraces, punishment. It is between us and
ourselves. It is alleviated or mitigated by acts of expiation. Consider
the most endearing of Jane Austen's heroines, Emma Woodhouse.
She has just been chastised by Mr. Knightly for being unkind to an
admittedly boring and garrulous elderly woman: "How could you be
so insolent in your wit to a woman of her character, age, and situation? Emma, I had not thought it possible."[3] Emma blushes, tries to
laugh it off, and attempts to apologize, but before she has an opportunity, Mr. Knightly leaves. The frustration at not having the opportunity to acknowledge her wrongdoing leaves her feeling progressively

more guilty. "Never had she felt so agitated, mortified, grieved at any circumstance in her life. . . . The truth of his representation there was no denying. She felt it at her heart. How could she have been so brutal, so cruel to Miss Bates!. . . Time did not compose her. As she reflected more, she seemed to feel it more."

Poor Emma. All the pleasures of the day seemed only to compound her misery and wretchedness. But finally comfort does come; she discovers expiation! While a whole morning of would-be pleasures caused misery, "a whole evening of backgammon with her father was felicity to it. *There*, indeed, lay real pleasure, for there she was giving up the sweetest hours of the twenty-four to his comfort." This is the turning point for this indomitable young woman, and she proceeds to move from guilt to determination.

> Miss Bates should never happen again—no never! If attention in future could do away with past she might hope to be forgiven. She had often been remiss, her conscience told her so; remiss, perhaps, more in thought than fact; scornful, ungracious. But it should be so no more. In the warmth of true contrition she would call upon her the very next morning and it should be the beginning, on her side, of a regular, equal, kindly intercourse.[4]

When guilt is sufficiently extreme, there exists such self-disgust and self-contempt that even the expiation of punishment will not alleviate it. Chekhov expresses it beautifully in this short passage, in which Olga Ivanovna is married to a virtuous man who has been a kind and good husband to her. She has been unfaithful to him and she is now watching him die of diphtheria.

> Olga Ivanovna sat in her room and reflected that God was punishing her for deceiving her husband. That silent, uncomplaining, inexplicable man—impersonified, it seemed, on his sofa and suffered alone, uttering no groan. . . . She no longer thought of the moonlight Volga night, the love avowal, the romance of life in the peasant's hut; she remembered only that from caprice and selfishness she had smeared herself from head to feet with something vile and sticky which no washing would wash away.[5]

It is interesting that guilt is so often related as being contaminated, fouled, marked, soiled, or, as with Lady Macbeth, stained. But like Lady Macbeth, it is all the more typically guilt when the stain is only visible to ourselves.

Guilt is the most personal of emotions. It is internalized and intensely so. Fear and anger can be seen; they can be hidden assuredly, but when intense enough, they can be seen. Guilt cannot always be interpreted.

Guilt is also exclusively a human emotion. Guilty fear is obviously not. It is most evident in household pets. I have had more trouble with my wife and daughters over the one relatively unimportant point of whether animals can experience an emotion such as guilt. In the dozens of times my wife has come across this section, she is offended by the assertion that animals never feel guilty, and inevitably offers as proof the behavior of a disreputable dog, one Mr. Dooley. Dooley is a Kerry blue terrier and, as such, has all the expansiveness of the Irish and rambunctiousness of his terrier breeding. He is therefore constantly, but only metaphorically, "in the doghouse." That slinky, slippery, slithering, ingratiating, tail-between-the-legs, whimpering, and altogether disgusting behavior which follows his typical outrage is, my wife and children are convinced, the ultimate expression of guilt. It inevitably reduces them to a state of forgiveness—and amnesia. Gone is the outrage and out comes the sympathy. His miserable behavior being interpreted as guilt, and therefore implying contrition, demands forgiveness.

I, on the other hand, remain unconvinced because I have never noticed Dooley approaching me "asking" to be punished. If anything, quite the contrary. I know immediately when he has violated the code of canine conduct. He is nowhere to be found, hiding under, in, or behind some barricade. I have never found that this presumed "guilty" feeling and behavior have been diminished by punishment, nor has the behavior been compounded by love, as guilt would be. But my family remains unconvinced. I have resorted to the one-upmanship of quoting "higher sources," among whom who could be higher than Martin Buber? In his discussion on guilt, he states:

> Conscience means to us the capacity and tendency of man radically to distinguish between those of his past and future actions which should be approved and those which should be disapproved. . . . Conscience can, naturally, distinguish and if necessary condemn . . . not merely deeds but also omissions, not

merely decisions but also failures to decide, indeed even images and wishes that have just arisen or are remembered. . . . One must bear in mind that among all living beings known to us, *man alone* is able to set at a distance not only his environment but also himself. As a result, he becomes for himself a detached object about which he can not only "reflect," but which he can from time to time confirm as well as condemn.[6]

One would think that psychoanalysis would have early dealt with the concept of guilt, but it did not. Freud was long in discovering a way to integrate guilt into conscience mechanism. As early as the 1890s, Freud was aware that certain counterforces kept our natural drives for pleasure in check. He correctly located them in the emotions well before he was prepared to elaborate any theory of conscience. He referred to the feelings of shame, disgust, revulsion, and loathing as counter forces that limited and controlled our drives for pleasure.

His first full attempt to deal with conscience did not occur until 1913 when he wrote *Totem and Taboo*. Building on his recognition that group living was an essential survival mechanism for the individual, Freud concluded that certain conscience mechanisms could not be simply learned anew in each generation, but were essentially part of the genetic nature of the human being. Conscience here was still regulated by fear and still was always, inevitably oriented toward the figure of authority. We acted as though the punitive parent were within us and therefore cognizant of all our wrongdoing. The controller—even though within us—was always some other, some punishing figure. Good behavior then served the purposes of avoiding punishment and retaliation. The only mechanism visualized at this time was guilty fear, and the driving force that kept us from selfishly pursuing individual aims was an internalized image of the father. Later, that all-knowing presence of power and authority would be assigned to God—or Father in Heaven.

That marvelous modern moralist Philip Roth has young Portnoy visualize this by seeing women authority figures as his ubiquitous mother.

She was so deeply imbedded in my consciousness that for the first year of school I seem to have believed that each of my teachers was my mother in disguise. As soon as the last bell had sounded, I would rush off for home, wondering as I ran if I could possibly make it to our apartment before she had succeeded in transforming herself. Invariably she was already in the kitchen by the time I arrived, and setting out my milk and cookies. Instead of causing me to give up my delusions, however, the feat merely intensified my respect for her powers. And then it was always a relief not to have caught her between incarnations anyway—even if I never stopped trying. . . . The burden of betrayal that I imagined would fall to me if I ever came upon her unawares was more than I wanted to bear at the age of five. I think I even feared that I might have to be done away with were I to catch sight of her flying in from school through the bedroom window, or making herself emerge, limb by limb, out of an invisible state and into her apron. . . . Of course, when she asked me to tell her all about my day at kindergarten, I did so scrupulously. I didn't pretend to understand all the implications of her ubiquity, but that it had to do with finding out the kind of little boy I was when I thought she wasn't around—that was indisputable. One consequence of this fantasy, which survived (in this particular form) into the first grade, was that seeing as I had no choice, I became honest.[7]

According to this view of conscience, we behave well because whether the punitive parent is present or not, we have the sense of him within us. We assume that, like the view of God entertained by some children, the parent is an omniscient Peeping Tom, who in seeing all is prepared to expose all, and punish the same.

Later, as Freud became more and more involved with the concept of identification, leading him close but never quite to the point of discovering love, he began to acknowledge a distinction between guilt and guilty fear. Identification became the vehicle for incorporating guilt into the processes of conscience.

Identification is a peculiar phenomenon. We have all experienced it. It is, in great part, what makes you, whether you like it or not, like your parent—at least in certain respects. Identification is seen as literally internalizing—swallowing up—another person and his attributes, or, if not that person, some idealized image of the way you thought he was, or the way he ought to have been.

Identification becomes a marvelous device for learning that shortcuts all the small experiences of tedious conditioning. It is not imitation, although it may lead to it. It is much more an unconscious and unwilled process. Identification leads to manners, form, taste, attitudes—all of the behavior that makes little English boys seem so English and French boys so precociously Gallic. The same procedure allows us to incorporate a model of proper moral behavior. This model exists—in our unconscious, unbeknownst to our conscious self—as an ideal against which we will measure ourselves. This ego ideal becomes fundamental to the self-respect mechanisms of the individual. In this final conception of conscience Freud continues to be impressed with the importance of guilty fear and the internalized parent, but in addition he postulates that there is an internalized ideal of behavior by which we, our actual selves (our Ego), judge our own behavior—and in our failures experience true guilt. Guilt, then, is a form of self-disappointment. It is the sense of anguish that we did not achieve our standards of what we ought to be. We have fallen short. We have somehow or other betrayed some internal sense of potential self. This is why guilt is the most internalized and personal of emotions. You-against-you allows no buffer—and no villains except oneself. Even when guilty fear is internalized, it is as if someone else were there. But with guilt, our internal structure feels torn apart. This is why guilt is so painful to endure.

Guilt is thus *not* a "useless" emotion; it is the emotion that shapes so much of our goodness and generosity. It signals us when we have transgressed from codes of behavior that we personally want to sustain. Feeling guilty informs us that we have failed our own ideals. As Paul Ricoeur has so eloquently stated:

> Guilt becomes a way of putting oneself before a sort of invisible tribunal which measures the offense, pronouncing the condemnation, and inflicts the punishment; at the extreme point of interiorization, moral consciousness is a look which watches, judges, and condemns; the sentiment of guilt is therefore the consciousness of being inculcated and incriminated by this interior tribunal.[8]

The readiness to avoid the emotion testifies to the discomfort and therefore the driving force of the feeling. To avoid it, we may avoid the behavior that generates it—or, short of that, expiate it. At times the avoidance takes the form of an almost childish avoidance. This results in the "hot-potato" game, which probably leads to more domestic quarreling than any other emotion.

It is much easier to feel anger than guilt. As a result, when something goes wrong, there is often an immediate tendency to attribute fault to some other—to protect against its being assigned to us. The irony is that even when there is no fault at all, we defensively assume "someone" must be to blame—for the car breakdown, the canceled performance, the rained-out picnic. "If *you* hadn't told me. . . ." "I told you we should have. . . ." "*You* had to insist on. . . ." The fear that the guilt will be passed on to oneself often makes us angry with whoever happens to be sharing the scene of the accident. A typical example of the hot-potato syndrome, whereby guilt is converted into blame, is the following. The husband is going out to mail a letter. On the way to mailing the letter he will pass a grocery store. Wife to husband: "Would you mind picking up a quart of milk?" Husband to wife: "Certainly not. I'm passing right by." Husband goes to post office; stops at grocery store; buys the milk; leaves his wallet on the counter. On the way home he realizes the loss and goes back—no wallet.

He has his choice then. He can feel guilty for having done something "stupid," i.e., wrong. It is he who has betrayed himself and he will feel guilty. It is not guilty fear. No one is going to punish him. (I am here assuming a gentle and loving wife.) More often than not, however, the husband will come home not with contrition or guilt but with a "You and your damn milk" comment.

This phenomenon is so universal it is possible to see it when even a no-fault chance event occurs. Because of the fear that somehow we may have had some responsibility, because of the readiness of certain people to assume guilt for almost any disaster, we defensively fix responsibilities somewhere other than ourselves even where no responsibility is involved. For the most part these maneuvers prove ineffectual. We feel the guilt; we have been—even if only in our anxious illusions—responsible for a wrong.

It is obvious, then, that guilt is of a different order of emotion from fear. Fear and rage, as Cannon pointed out, are emotions oriented to the survival of the organism. They serve one as an individual, or at least they did in the days before civilization. In the primitive society there was predator and prey. In that struggle for survival the emotion (fear or rage) signaled whether it was appropriate to flee or fight. Guilt seems so unself-serving, so peculiar an emotion. But it is not alone among the emotions in its other-serving goals.

Love is not (or should not be) a singular activity, and is also an unselfish emotion. It involves communication between people and, as such, involves reciprocity. What survival purpose is served by emotions like guilt, love, and caring? Would we not survive more adequately if, unencumbered by such emotions, we fought for each scrap of food even to the point of personal greed and gluttony and the starvation of our weaker neighbor?

The conscience mechanisms and the emotions that serve them testify that for *Homo sapiens* community is not an ideal but a biological necessity. There is no such thing as individual survival. The human being is human because of the nurture of other human beings and, missing this, will not survive. If the love and caring are supplied only minimally, he may survive as a biological entity without the qualities of humanness that elevate him above the common animal host. If at any key point an individual is withdrawn from contact with his kind, he may recreate social relationships in his imagination that sustain him for a time, but he suffers the risk of being reduced to an animal indistinguishable from lower forms.

We are so constructed that we must serve the social good—on which we are dependent for our own survival—and when we do not, we suffer the pangs of guilt. In that sense guilt parallels the sex drive. Here one sees the most primitive, the most central and essential fusion between individual pleasure and group needs. Pleasure and procreation are bound so intensely together that even while the individual serves his own pleasure he guarantees the survival of the species. Similarly, guilt and its fellow emotions of caring, loving, shame, compassion, empathy, and pity bind us to those who are needed for our own survival. Guilt may thus be recognized as a guardian of our goodness, calling us back from unhealthy self-absorption to an awareness of the social fabric to which we belong.

NOTES

1. Book review of "The Psychopathic God: Adolf Hitler," by Robert G. L. Waite, *The New Yorker*, Aug. 29, 1977, p. 84.

2. *The Woman Warrior: Memoirs of a Girlhood among Ghosts* (New York: Alfred A. Knopf, 1977), pp. 197, 198, 199.

3. *Emma,* in *The Complete Novels of Jane Austen* (New York: Random House, Modern Library), p. 992.

4. Ibid., p. 993.

5. Anton Chekhov, "La Cigale," in *The Stories of Anton Chekhov* (New York: Modern Library, 1932), p. 99.

6. Quoted in *The Knowledge of Man,* ed. M. Friedman (London: George Allen & Unwin, 1965), p. 133; italics mine.

7. *Portnoy's Complaint* (New York: Random House, 1967), pp. 3, 4.

8. "Guilt, Ethics and Religion," in *Conscience: Theological and Psychological Perspectives* (New York: Newman Press, 1973), pp. 15, 16.

Rationality distinguishes "humans" from "persons." It is that unique power which "reflects upon, judges, and places the other elements of our nature. Persons are "beings that can rationally understand their lives and comprehend the possiblility of moral responsibility. . . . " Reason "gives us the capacity to array, weigh, and choose among all imaginable, possible values," among these the ability to choose whether to extend further our power over our bodies and the earth.

REASON   H. Tristram Engelhardt

We humans are recurrently puzzled by ourselves and about ourselves. We are often driven to measuring our capacities in order to gain a picture of who and what we are. This puzzling about ourselves as much as anything marks us as humans. When it takes its serious forms, such puzzling reveals us as beings employing concepts and arguments as best we can to frame views of ourselves. It is rationality that reflects upon, judges, and places the other elements of our natures. However, rationality is an important topic only as an entrée to understanding why being a person is not the same thing as being human. Rationality reaches beyond the mere particulars of our humanity.

By persons is meant rational beings, beings that are self-possessing through concepts, beings that can call themselves their own. A person is thus a being that can say, "I did this," "I thought this," "I am doing this," "I am thinking this." As Kant noted, it can unite its experiences and actions under an "I think," and know that it so unifies itself.[1] This is a cardinal power of reason and a necessary element of persons. This power allows persons to regard, and then accept or reject, the particular characteristics that may mark them as humans. Persons can, as a result, have a position regarding their very nature and accept or reject it in whole or in part. Human characteristics thus receive a place in the lives of persons. In this sense, being a person is the higher or real truth or significance of being human, to use a Hegelian turn of phrase.[2] In attempting to give an account of what it is to be a human, one ends up by giving an account of what it means to be a person, and the two are not equivalent.[3] To understand what it is to be a human forces one to conceive of oneself as a rational being judging, and possibly altering, one's own characteristics and nature. As a result, the meaning of being a human is not denied but recast in more ample, more embracing terms.

This is likely to sound mysterious, metaphysical, and opaque. However, I hope to dispel the mystery and, in part at least, allow the light of analytic thought to shine through by examining the interplay between the meaning of being a person and being a human. Since I take rationality to be a necessary element of being a person, this will bring me to my treatment of rationality. It is in this fashion that I will sketch the role of rationality in our nature as persons and approach the puzzle concerning the character of the powers that make us human. However, in the process, I will be rephrasing the mission itself. I will be suggesting that the powers of reason, those powers which most truly mark us as the beings we are, show us that we are not simply humans. Being a person is, as suggested above, more than being human. Thus this inquiry will be more toward exploring those powers that characterize us as persons than those powers that characterize us as humans.

In developing this argument, I will be forwarding a view of ourselves that has implications for our judgments concerning various technological possibilities for our own self-creation. As one would expect, many of the examples of such self-creation lie in biomedicine. As the arguments unfold, I am sure that one will note an indebtedness to the thought of Hegel[4] and a congeniality with some of the remarks of Robert Nozick.[5] It will as well be apparent that I concur with many of the conclusions and proposals of arguments by Joseph Fletcher on points bearing on contraception, *in vitro* fertilization, and other examples of man recasting the rationales of his body through technology.[6] By developing this position I will, therefore, be in disagreement with contrary arguments made by others such as Paul Ramsey.[7] I will be supporting the virtues, or at least the lack of intrinsic viciousness, in our self-creation as rational animals.

In speaking of reason, I mean the capacity to frame, through ideas, concepts or notions, grounds for or against avenues of conduct or opinions. Reason thus shows itself when we state who we are, what our interests are, and what our concerns are. By reason I mean, then, not just the power to discourse but to discourse with oneself, to call oneself as well as others to account, to hold an argument knowingly with oneself. Reason in this sense includes the powers of knowing, of being conscious, and of choosing. Reason is, therefore, the capacity to know self-consciously. It is the power to know and to know that one knows. In short, it is meant with all the weight that reason must bear in the term "rational animal," or in Sir Edward Coke's definition of murder as the killing of a "reasonable creature in being, and under the King's peace."[8]

Reason in this sense is the essence of persons. All things that are rational in this fashion are moral agents. They are the beings that one can always think of as members of Kant's moral community, his *mundus intelligibilis*.[9] They, being self-conscious and able to choose knowingly, can be held responsible for their actions and are therefore worthy of blame and praise. They are, then, moral agents, the constituents of any possible moral community such as Kant's *corpus mysticum* of rational beings.[10] They are bearers of rights and duties. One may need to add as well that they must have the ability to comprehend the notion of rights and duties, to envisage the possibility of having a view of the good, as is reflected in John Rawl's argument that moral persons are distinguished by (1) a capacity to have a rational plan of life, and (2) a sense of justice.[11] Depending on how much is packed into the second condition, one might suspect that Rawls has described not simply moral agents but morally inclined moral agents. In any event, beings that can rationally understand their lives and comprehend the possibility of moral responsibility are persons.

This is not, however, only a sufficient condition for being a person. It is a necessary condition as well. An entity that is not capable of being worthy of blame and praise, that is not responsible for its actions, that is not a moral agent, would not be a person in the sense of a member of the moral community, the *mundus intelligibilis*. This follows from the fact that the notion of a moral community based not on force, but rather on respect of freedom, presupposes such beings.

One could, all else being equal, destroy other entities without their consent without violating the notion of a moral community.

Rationality, the Moral Community, and Human Nature

By exploring the notion of a moral community of persons, as an intellectual standpoint through which one can understand moral obligations, one can better appreciate the concept of persons and the grounds for accenting the rational nature of persons. This sense of the moral community arises as one explores what is involved in rational beings jointly considering moral issues. If one wishes to conceive of the possibility of resolving disputes concerning the nature of proper lines of conduct and of proper choices of goods, without recourse to force, then one must envisage, as an intellectual device, a community of individuals asking ethical questions and resolving them while giving mutual respect of freedom. The ideas of respect of persons and of persons as moral agents are integral to the notion of such a possible practice.

This also should not be interpreted as a mystical, mysterious, or metaphysical claim. Rather, this notion of a moral community is based on an entreaty to consider what general practices can be entertained by rational beings with respect to the resolution of moral conflicts. In one such practice (1) one asks questions about moral issues and then resolves them by an appeal to reasons or by some other common agreement, and (2) one blames all those who refuse to participate in this practice, for such a practice is *the* enterprise for the peaceful negotiation of moral issues. Any individual who refuses to participate, who reserves the right to use force against the innocent for his or her own ends, cannot be held to be anything but worthy of blame by members of a community of rational beings based on mutual respect of freedom. The moral community as a community of beings resolving issues by mutual negotiation, not force, is then an intellectual possibility. In an intellectual argument about how to resolve moral disputes, appeal to such a notion is the clincher in the debate with the greatest scope and force. That is, *if* one is asking questions about how to resolve moral issues as rational issues (and is not asking how to force others into agreement), or (an alternate formulation) one is asking how one can resolve moral disputes about what counts as proper conduct without recourse to force, *then* one will need to conceive of oneself as a member of a community of rational beings bound mutually to respect each other's freedom in the debate. The central sanction of such a community will be that of blameworthiness. Anyone who embraces this possibility ought to hold those who use unconsented-to force against another to be worthy of blame, even if that force serves to bring one person to do what another person believes is proper for him. That one may be interested in imposing one's view of the good life upon another is likely. However, such cannot be tolerated by those entertaining this general moral notion of what ethical reflection and discussion involves as a practice: reason giving and negotiation, not force.

If, however, individuals claim to know what goods others should embrace, and then impose those goods (e.g., valuing freedom above other goods, or pleasing the Deity as the highest good), that commitment to force (1) excludes such individuals from the peaceable community of moral agents, (2) authorizes all peaceable beings to defend others from such value imperialists, (3) removes from such imperialists the claim to respect as innocent, free beings (although they may claim respect not as free individuals but because of interest in maximizing freedom, or pleasure to the Deity—one might imagine, for example, such individuals using force to prevent rational individuals from committing suicide in order to preserve their future freedom), and (4) commits such value imperialists to the very difficult-to-defend proposition that they, in fact, know what the good for the other is.

There is thus a libertarian constraint upon the peaceable moral community in that it is based upon freedom as a side constraint, not freedom as a value. It is committed to exploring ethical conflicts peacefully. It therefore need make no claim to knowledge of what is good for others. It is founded on a weaker but more general claim: the notion of the moral community as based on mutual respect, not force. It envisages a possible irresolvable pluralism of views of the good. It is not committed to any particular good, not even freedom as a value. It is instead committed to procedures that are attempts peacefully to negotiate diverse moral institutions. It relies only on interest in ethical debate, on raising ethical questions as intellectual questions among equals. It is for this reason that it eschews force. Freedom is a side constraint for its members in the sense that they

must recognize mutual rights to forbearance as a condition for the
possibility for conceiving of such a community of rational beings.
This view of a moral community and its members thus allows for a
matrix of rights and duties which are not reducible to interests in
goods and values but which are rather recognized as a condition for
such a moral realm. One thus is offered a way of conceiving of a non-
consequentialist moral framework within which free individuals
can attempt mutually to discover, invent, create, or decide upon
common visions of the good, and therefore teleological understandings of the good life. Such consequentialist or teleological views are,
however, domesticated. They are placed within the constraints of respecting freedom. They cannot license imposing an orthodoxy.

This view of a moral community reveals persons as reasoning,
puzzling beings who need not be humans. The members of this
moral community include not only gods and angels but possibly rational chimpanzees and dolphins, as well as all rational extraterres-
trial beings who may exist. That is, insofar as one invokes the idea of
a community of peaceable, rational beings, one does not include simply humans. In fact, inclusion is by no means based upon membership in the human race. Rather, one is included because one is a rational being who in reflection can freely choose, and therefore whose
freedom could not be abridged without offending the notion of such
a community. It is in terms of such a notion that one would understand clearly the immoralities of shooting an innocent, rational
being from another planet as a clear and unequivocal violation of the
most basic and general framework of morality. Such an action is
much clearer in its moral significance than is infanticide or abortion,
which do not involve killing a rational being.[12] The members of the
mundus intelligibilis of Kant, the denizens of John Rawls's original
position, need not be humans. They must, however, be persons in
Kant's sense. Kant, for example, argued that "rational nature is distinguished from others in that it proposes an end to itself,"[13] that "it
follows incontestably that every rational being must be able to regard
himself as an end in himself with reference to all laws to which he may
be subject, whatever they may be, and thus as giving universal law."[14]

However, if, unlike Kant, one does not hold that one can discover a
compelling, concrete view of the good life, one is forced to be an ethical subjectivist within the bounds of respecting freedom as a side

constraint, not freedom as a value. (1) Insofar as one takes Hegel's and others' criticisms of Kant seriously,[15] namely, that Kant provided universalistic matrices without content, and (2) insofar as one does not hold that one can univocally discover the good for humans, much less persons, one will then see the moral community as setting the framework within which one will peaceably invent or create a concrete, moral life. The more that one believes that the failure to establish a universal human ethic as well as the failure to establish a method for its discovery is due not to a lack of effort or sincerity but to the divergent ways in which humans can and do envisage the good life, then the more one will justifiably despair that any appeal to ideal observers, however well situated, or to groups of rational contractors, however disinterested, will be successful in establishing such an ethic. One will conclude that individuals invent more or less encompassing, more or less coherent, and more or less rich views of the good life. One will then entertain the possibility that there will be numerous, plausible, but incompatible views of the good life. As long as they include respect of persons, there will not be strong moral arguments to establish the validity or invalidity of the various rival views.

Even the fact that nearly all humans agree concerning a particular good, while only a few take exception, will prove nothing with regard to whether the deviant few ought or ought not to agree. It will prove only that they are not like most humans. One might, for example, imagine trying to resolve the issues of whether it is morally better to live the life of a homosexual or a heterosexual, to engage in or not to engage in duelling, to suffer bravely through protracted terminal illness or to seek rational escape as a Seneca would have through suicide. One will be at best driven to portraying styles of life and indicating that some allow some virtues to flourish and give short shrift to other virtues, while other lifestyles allow different virtues to flourish and fail to support the pursuit of others. In short, one will be driven to a subjectivist view of the concrete moral life, and to holding that humans can achieve only some of the many possible human virtues, and that the choice of a particular lifestyle involves choosing to which of such sets of virtues one will give one's energies. One might use the metaphor of a mosaic in which one orders the various human goods to create a rich pattern. Many rich patterns will be open to development within the bounds of respecting the freedom of persons. One's choice among them will be made more on aesthetic than on ethical grounds.

This means that when persons come to reflect upon their inclinations and drives, they may not only imagine different orderings of the merits of those inclinations and drives but also in fact alter those inclinations and drives. That is, persons may entertain the possibility of manipulating, altering, or changing their nature in ways to allow the achievement of goods that would not be possible in the pre-manipulated state. One's understanding of the good life, and one's fantasies as a person, may move one to set aside various of the most human inclinations.

After all, humans are moved by aggressive passions, by lustful inclinations, and by dispositions to greed. This list of usual human passions and inclinations is unlikely to command uncritical approval. Thus, if one concludes that there are inborn inclinations to aggression which culminate in human wars, and are in that sense a part of human nature, one is likely to conclude as well that, all else being equal, it would be good if those elements of human nature could be appropriately changed, manipulated, or tampered with so as to render us a more pacific species. Or for that matter, because the strong drive to heterosexual intercourse has contributed to a dangerous overpopulation of the earth, one may be brought to reflect that it would be good if humans could be brought to assign equal or greater value to oral intercourse, mutual masturbation, or homosexual activities so as to effect a decline in population, without force but with pleasurable assent. In short, different reasonable individuals are likely to take exception to any list of the characteristics of human nature, or of the usual activities of humans, and seek grounds for modifying or altering them.

The Powers That Make Us Human

It is unlikely that one will be able to produce a univocal account of human nature or of the human good. The initial difficulty will be in specifying what one means by human with respect to our species or for that matter our genus as it has evolved and changed over time. If for purposes of discussion one limits one's consideration to the species *Homo sapiens* in the twentieth century, difficulties will still abound. One might consider, for example, how one would characterize the significance of being human. One approach would be to consider the *taxonomic locus* of the human genus or species. The genus *Homo* shares with the genera *Ramapithecus* and *Australopithecus* membership in the family Hominidae of the suborder Anthropoidea of the order primates of the class Mammalia. In signaling what distinguishes humans, one would need to indicate the properties that mark primates. For example, primates have limbs that are unusually long and pentadactyl hands and feet that are relatively large. One would want to note that Anthropoidea show a tendency to walk upright and an increased specialization of the nervous system, a specialization that becomes marked in the Hominidae. With respect to the Hominidae family, one would want to stress the development of tool-making capacity, language, and other symbol-related or dependent behaviors. One would do so, however, without holding that these characteristics are necessarily unique to Hominidae. Aside from the obvious possibility that species on other planets may have evolved to be tool makers and to use language, at least the rudiments of such capacities appear to exist in other members of the suborder Anthropoidea. In short, one either characterizes humans in terms of their peculiar anatomical structures and physiological capacities, or describes them in terms that are likely to be characteristic of persons as such. Indicating that humans are tool-using or symbol-using animals is probably simply to characterize them as rational animals, and not to forward any properties that would distinguish the species *Homo sapiens* as such. In fact, such criteria would be of unambiguous usefulness for assigning species membership only on planets where just one species had developed rational capacities. One could, however, surely imagine circumstances under which such would not be the case.

There is, however, another tack that one could take. One might argue that the mosaic of emotions, drives, and instincts that mark humans is unique to humans insofar as they are functions of human cerebral anatomy and human anatomy in general. However, one would expect that there would also be great similarity in the feelings of joy, fear, anger, lust, and love among all mammals insofar as they share similar limbic cortical structures. These similarities would be more pronounced as cerebral similarities are greater, as in the case of higher primates. Yet one would expect some differences due to such feelings, as well as a startling difference due to such feelings and drives being made a part of the life of persons, beings who reflect upon and thus alter the significance of all their experiences.

One might want to borrow Kant's metaphor of concepts and intuitions to indicate that all rational animals must receive content for their lives from the passions, instincts, and drives that their bodies provide. Without such, the life of reason would be empty.[16] However, only when such passions, drives, and instincts are placed within the realm of rationality do they cease to be blind. In fact, then they become less idiosyncratic and open to (at least in principle) vague comparisons with the emotions that possible different species of rational animals might possess. However, the content itself would likely retain a special mark of incommunicability. The language of human passions is likely to be open only to other humans or, at best, to other primates with similar neural structures. For example, to explain to members of a different species of rational animals what it is like to have the feelings that we have when particular parts of our nervous system are excited would probably entail crossing a more insurmountable gulf than that of explaining to a man born blind what color is like, or to envisage what a rational, speech-endowed bee could tell us of the properties of ultraviolet light. One might in the end understand what such experiences are like, though one could not imagine them.

The notion of members of other rational species has been appealed to as an intellectual fulcrum by which to move us from a parochial understanding of what it means to be a person and toward a more appropriate understanding of what one could mean by talking of humans. In many of the questions in bioethics, such distinctions are of crucial significance. One might think of issues such as the definition of death or the morality of abortion, of possible abortifacient devices such as IUDs, or of fetal research. Greatly confused questions are often asked, such as when does the fetus become alive or become human, or when does the brain-dead individual cease to be a human. Probably in most of these instances what is meant, or should be meant, is when do fetuses become persons, or when, due to brain damage, do human individuals cease to be persons. Living human sperm, ova, zygotes, embryos, and fetuses are all examples of human life. They are not simian, porcine, equine, or canine. The issue is when in our life cycle, which embraces both haploid and diploid forms, it is appropriate to speak of human life as also constituting the life of a person. The same is true at the end of the human life cycle. A brain-dead but otherwise alive human individual may continue to show many important characteristics of life and species membership, including the capacity to be cross-fertile with other humans, though he has ceased to be a person. In addition, one is likely to discover that in many moral debates one is presuming more than one concept of person. That complexity, however, need not be explored here. It is enough to indicate that the core sense of person, that of being a rational individual, is not the same as that of being a human.[17]

This conclusion is of cardinal significance in understanding the question, "What are the powers that make us human?" It is *a fortiori* of importance in conceiving the proper answers. If one, for example, approaches the question as that of identifying what would mark us as the particular species we are, one will get quite different answers than if one understands the question as one of identifying the properties that mark persons. One may, in fact, receive a third set of answers based on understanding "human" as an honorific term that identifies an individual as excelling in certain virtues and powers. Thus, when one says, "Voilà un homme," one should probably not be understood as applying a taxonomy, identifying a particular organism as human. So also it would probably be inappropriate to interpret this as discovering a person. Rather, one is likely indicating an individual who is a *real* human, or a *real* person in the sense of bearing special qualities and distinctions that we esteem highly. Finally, one may really be talking about persons or rational animals.

Mixtures of these four genre are seen in traditional lists of the powers that make us human. Thus mortality would indicate a property unique not to humans but to all rational animals. Hope might come closer to identifying a capacity dependent upon a nervous system of a particular sort and therefore distinctly human. The same can be said of many virtues when specified very concretely. They will also mark human in the honorific sense. However, autonomy, responsibility, and justice could be framed in terms of persons as such. One sees this, for example, in Kant's writings when he indicates that he is delineating a morality for rational beings as such, not merely humans.[18] Autonomy, responsibility, the capacity for choice, and the ability to act justly can be sketched without restricting them to members of the species *Homo sapiens*. It is surely the case that they will receive their content through the kinds of lives that the members of a species can live. Feelings will undoubtedly be most species-specific in that they are likely to turn on peculiarities of a nervous system.

As a result, to attempt to delineate the powers that make us human will drive one either to delineating in greater detail the idiosyncrasies of the members of the species *Homo sapiens*, or to analyzing what is embraced in the notion of a rational animal. One approach focuses on the idiosyncrasies of a species, the other upon those qualities that would make us brothers and sisters of rational animals anywhere in this cosmos, and half-siblings of angels and the gods. It will only be by pursuing both that we can frame an adequate view of our powers.

Further, the fact that we understand and judge the idiosyncrasies of our nature as humans in terms of what we as rational beings take to be sensible has important implications for our understandings of ourselves. As a consequence, our intraspecies variations will, all else being equal, need to be regarded simply as that, variations. There will be nothing ineluctably normative in the inclinations, dispositions, attractions, and interests that most humans have, so that minority, abnormal, deviant, or unusual inclinations, sentiments, or behaviors can be judged as wrong on that basis alone. We as rational beings will need in the end to judge whether, and in what respect, such inclinations are reasonable and proper considering (1) the goals we as rational individuals wish conjointly to pursue, and (2) our interests to live in a moral community bound together by mutual respect, not force. Thus the evidence that the great apes are disposed to set border guards between their territories and to beat intruders viciously will not lead us to the conclusion that such is "normal'" primate and human behavior, and is therefore moral.[19] Or, to return to an earlier example, one will not be able to conclude from what most individuals believe or are inclined to do, whether it would be wrong or proper to attempt (with the consent of those involved) to gain greater acceptance of "abnormal" sexual practice as a way of solving the world population problems. One would need, for instance, to weigh the merits of proposals to expand the acceptability of oral intercourse or homosexual activity to control population growth in terms of their implications for the various goods and values that persons have chosen to pursue. In such assays, one would naturally have to take into consideration the capacities and usual inclinations of members of the species *Homo sapiens*. Though the capacities of the species pose limitations upon what rational animals can accomplish, they do not impose binding moral laws.

We as rational animals can step back from our usual inclinations and decide which of them we wish to have prosper, and which to have muted or extirpated. Science through technology is likely to offer us opportunities to give reality to judgments that would otherwise remain fantasies. One will surely need to pursue such Promethean goals with caution and prudence. The realm of morality for persons is, after all, constituted by the requirement of mutual respect of free choice and by the prudential goal that one ought to maximize the goods and values that one and one's community esteem.

Beyond that, it will not be feasible to identify *normal* humans in an evaluative sense by an act of discovery alone. Species do not have a conceptual unity or essence that their members ought to embody. Instead they are, at least in the case of sexually reproducing species, potentially interbreeding populations that change in their characteristics through time. Species are marked by members showing differing variations, each with differing survival values, given different environments. Indeed, as rational individuals we are not only free to choose the environment in terms of which successful adaptation, and therefore normality and deviance, is to be tested, but we may choose the goals of adaptation themselves. Therefore, no one variation will be normative *sub species aeternitates*. Nor will one goal or set of goals be binding. We need not, for example, value species survival as the highest good. One could imagine the members of the human species deciding to reproduce no further, and instead to have a final luxurious period in which the resources of earth would be consumed. Freedom, and in that strong sense morality, would not have been violated. It is only that we do not anticipate that most humans would indeed agree to such goals.

Reason: The Power That Makes Us Persons

It is reason that gives us the capacity to array, weigh, and choose among all imaginable, possible values. It is this that distinguishes reason as our cardinal capacity. It gives a transcending sense and purpose to science and technology. It indicates the inescapably Promethean destiny of persons. Humans as persons can always reconceive their nature, view it in new fashions, and then by science through technology move to recast its very lineaments. Thus human persons are cast into a moral predicament. No longer can they turn to an understanding of their nature qua biological species for a source of moral values. Instead, their destiny is to create and invent their own values. It will never be possible simply to discover the good for humans. Reason, in short, creates our destiny as humans. We must choose, for example, the extent to which we will pursue capacities that outstrip what has ever been part of our nature or the nature of other animals.

This view need not necessarily lead one to particular moral views about particular issues. It will, however, change how one understands the significance of such views. One will, for example, see the development of contraception as an attempt to refashion our nature in the service of the goals we have as persons, independently of one's final judgment of the virtues and banes of contraception. Though other mammals, or indeed other primates, do not have volitional control over their fecundity, we have developed the ability through technology to set these limitations of nature aside. This has allowed a volitional separation of the social and recreational elements of sex from the biological dimensions of sex. This separation constitutes a radical refashioning of nature and a departure from the idiosyncrasies that we possess as members of a particular species in order to achieve goals that we embrace as rational animals, as persons. The development of adequate contraception is thus an excellent example of how we as persons create and fashion ourselves. In allowing sexual activity for pleasure and social reasons without reproductive consequences, we have changed the significance of social relations and conditions, including those of premarital and extramarital sex, as well as those of massive involvement of women in the work force of industrial countries, childless married couples, and the ability to control population growth.

Similar issues arise as well in many other technological developments in the biomedical sciences. One might think here of such simple procedures as artificial insemination by a donor. One might consider as well such current nascent technology as *in vitro* fertilization with embryo implantation. One might consider also more Promethean proposals such as those sketched in *Brave New World*.[20] Thus, for example, the proposal to abolish all motherhood[21] by the use of *in vitro* fertilization and gestation in order (1) to abolish all maternal morbidity and mortality, (2) to prevent effectively the birth of deformed infants (i.e. by timely decantation of maldeveloping embryos), and (3) to achieve a more ample equality between the sexes, would have to be weighed on its own merits. It would not be possible simply to discuss such proposals as unnatural or abnormal. Rather, persons would have to judge the likely benefits and risks involved, bearing in mind among the risks, the difficulties of assaying in advance the consequences of new technologies.

Reason thus marks us as beings who can in principle be free of the idiosyncrasies of our nature. We are destined to be self-fashioners. In that the biomedical sciences are intimately involved in understanding how we can in principle alter or modify our present natures, they are most likely to raise the tempting and disturbing questions that will haunt us in the future. We will not be able to retreat from such decisions by labeling them as violations of our human nature. We will rather have to seek those disciplines of restraint that will give us the prudence to engage successfully in our self-creation.

Conclusion

We find ourselves to be persons, rational animals, not simply humans. Our cardinal power—reason—marks us as not merely members of a particular species with its peculiarities. Instead, in self-reflection we transcend these roots. It is not possible adequately to characterize humans without noting that rationality is a singular capacity displayed by most members of the species. However, that very capacity, far from being a human idiosyncrasy or unique property, is the mark of persons generally. On the one hand, it is the basis of a moral bond with all persons who may exist, even if they are not humans. On the other hand, this human power gives us a perspective from which and through which human persons can judge and alter their humanity. Humanhood is thus put at the disposal of persons. The power of reason that marks us as humans makes us more than simply humans and seals us with a destiny of self-transcendence. In these Promethean promises of our biomedical technologies, we see intimations of this destiny. Far from being an alienating promise, it is a promise of a more personal future, a future in which our human idiosyncrasies may become less strange to the goals we as persons would choose. And should we as humans continue over a vast future to evolve, the continuity of our personhood will mark that future with a central unifying leitmotif that will not be found in the idiosyncrasies of human nature.[22]

The conceptual point is dialectical. To speak of ourselves as humans constrains us in the end to speak of ourselves as more than human. It forces us to different and conceptually richer notions. The quest to understand the powers that make us human leads inexorably to the quest to understand the powers that make us persons, and the cardinal one of these is reason.

NOTES

1. Immanuel Kant employs at least six senses of person or subject. See my "Kantian Knowledge of Other Persons—An Exploration," in *Akten des 4. Internationalen Kant-Kongresses Mainz* II.2 (Berlin: Walter de Gryter, 1974), pp. 576-81.

2. For Hegel, examining the concept of human leads to the concept of person, which is less idiosyncratic (e.g., gods, humans and angels can be persons) and more rationally explicable (i.e., the concept of person is a rational notion, not an empirical concept, a description of a particular species). In this sense, person is the higher truth of human. One needs to talk of persons in order to understand humans, but not humans in order to understand persons. See, for example, my *Mind-Body: A Categorical Relation* (The Hague: Martinus Nijhoff, 1973), pp. 92-104.

3. For a discussion of some of these issues, see Warner Becker, *Idealistische und materialistische Dialektik* (Stuttgart: Kohlhammer, 1970).

4. For example, I agree with Hegel that the moral of the ethical life is as much a historical, cultural creation as an intellectual discovery. See, for example, *The Philosophy of Right*, nos. 147, 150, and 343.

5. I concur in great proportion with Robert Nozick's distinction between

freedom as a value and freedom as a side constraint, and the importance of this distinction for understanding moral relations. See Robert Nozick, *Anarchy, State and Utopia* (New York: Basic Books, 1974), esp. pp. 30-35.

6. Joseph Fletcher, *Morals and Medicine* (Princeton, N. J.: Princeton University Press, 1979), ch. 7, pp. 211-25. There he holds that the fact that something is given by nature does not make it morally desirable or necessarily preferable to other options.

7. Paul Ramsey, "Shall We 'Reproduce'?," *Journal of the American Medical Association* 220 (June 5, 1972): 1346-50; 220 (June 12, 1972): 1480-85.

8. Sir Edward Coke, 3 *Institutes* 47.

9. Immanuel Kant, *Foundations of the Metaphysics of Morals*, Akademie ed., 4:438.

10. Kant, *Critique of Pure Reason*, A808-B836.

11. John Rawls, *A Theory of Justice* (Cambridge, Mass.: Belknap Press, 1971), p. 505.

12. Infants are, after all, not moral agents, although they are entities that have a high probability of becoming moral agents. See my "The Ontology of Abortion," *Ethics* 84:217-34; "Bioethics and the Process of Embodiment," *Perspectives in Biology and Medicine* 18:496-500; and "Ontology and Ontogeny," *The Monist* 60:15-28.

13. *Foundations of the Metaphysics of Morals*, trans. Lewis White Beck (Indianapolis: Bobbs-Merrill, 1959), p. 55. Akademie ed., 4:437.

14. Ibid. p. 56; Akademie ed., 4:438.

15. See, for example, Hegel's *Philosophy of Right*, no. 135 with Zusats, as well as Alasdair MacIntyre, *A Short History of Ethics* (New York: Macmillan, 1966), pp. 190-98.

16. Immanuel Kant, *Critique of Pure Reason*, B75.

17. That is, only some persons may be humans, and only some humans are persons in the strict sense I have outlined. Person does not include the properties that characterize human as biological species.

18. Kant in many places indicates that the ethic that he is describing applies to persons generally, not just humans. See, for example, *Foundations of the Metaphysics of Morals*, Akademie ed., 4:4-5, and *The Metaphysical Principles of Virtue*, Akademie ed., 6:223.

19. See, for example, *The Great Apes*, ed. David A. Hamburg and Elizabeth R. McCown (Menlo Park, Calif.: Benjamin Cummings, 1979).

20. Aldous Huxley, *Brave New World* (New York: Harper and Row, 1982).

21. See, for example, Edward Grossman, "The Obsolescent Mother," *Atlantic Monthly* 227 (May, 1971):39-50.

22. Olaf Stapledon gives a development of the human "species" or "genus" over a large span of time in what is a classic science fiction novel. There he portrays various remarkable biological forms that "humans" take during their history, which forms would not be denominated *Homo sapiens* by the usual taxonomy criteria, yet they are all persons. See *Last and First Men* (New York: Dover, 1968), originally published in 1939.

Sages and rulers from earliest times have struggled to understand the concept of justice, believing this quality to be a uniquely human and desirable trait. Why should we continue to care about justice? One can equate justice and morality, further defining "justice" as "essentially a matter of fair distribution." Justice, that is, is a problem of moral obligation. Distributive justice is preferable to equalitarian justice, particularly as one seeks to be just in the field of medicine. Distributive justice best serves society and the human.

JUSTICE   Joseph Fletcher

Why should we care about justice? Why should we bother about doing the right thing? The political answer is plain enough. Maintaining justice is necessary to a viable social order ("the rule of law"). In the international order the diplomatic answer is the same (the immunity of diplomatic personnel, for example). For individuals the answer is that acting justly is necessitated by enlightened self-interest—thus indicating, of course, that for pirates and assassins that particular reason lacks sufficient force. For the great majority of us the principle is: You respect his property or he won't respect yours.

According to ethical formalism, actions are moral if they satisfy norms or principles, whether there are expected benefits or not. The rational underpinning of this discussion, however, is ethical teleology, a position in which actions are morally validated by their consequences or "nonmoral" benefits. This clash is a classical issue, implicit or explicit in every ethical inquiry.

Moreover, in this discussion "justice" is synonymous with "fairness," not lawfulness. This is the way those early American patriots thought of justice when they engaged in civic disobedience at the Boston Tea Party of 1773, as a protest against Parliament's unfair trade laws. Just laws are just because they are fair, not because they are laws. The American Medical Association in 1973 dropped its code rule against passive euthanasia (i.e., stopping treatment) because it had to confess after a long history of stubbornness that it was

93

not fair to patients in cases of terminal illness. Laws—civil, criminal, professional, or moral—cannot stand up if experience shows us that their consequences are inhumane or unfair.

Since justice is a problem of ethics, i.e., of moral obligation, how are we to relate justice and morality? The grand tradition has always supposed them to be distinct, yet somehow tied together. Philosophers, theologians, and lawyers have treated them as different (albeit related) concepts. Close analysis reveals, however, that they are actually only two sides of the same thing: that as concepts they are coterminous and coinherent.

In this perspective if we speak of a just person, we mean that he or she acts morally; if we speak of a moral person, we mean one who acts justly. You cannot be just without being moral, nor moral without being just. Whenever the term "moral" is properly used, "justice" would do quite as well.

Kurt Baier commits a semantic error when he suggests that Plato in *The Republic* vitiated his examination of morality because he (Plato) failed to distinguish rightness and wrongness from justice—which Baier calls a "secondary notion."' Here we have an instance of assuming what needs to be shown. Plato's was a far more satisfactory view, upon analysis. Aristotle, too, spoke of the whole range of righteousness or moral concern as "general justice."

We find the same thing in the ancient Hebrews: as they saw it, essential justice and essential morality were one—conformity to the moral law. Justice was not merely one item among others "under" morality, one only of its forms. The Hebrews codified their morals just as they did their civil and criminal laws. (They believed, of course, that obligation came from the divine will, but this notion was religious, not ethical.) Put succinctly, behind and beneath both "morality" and "justice," the *idée mère* in all cultures is "do what is right, refuse what is wrong."

Christian ethics, following the later Greek philosophers, have always treated justice as one of the four cardinal virtues (the others being prudence, temperance, and fortitude), as if one could somehow be just without being prudent, temperate, or enduring. The logic of this quadripartite distinction entails preecisely that possibility, bizarre as it is. Mill, in *Utilitarianism* (chapter five), perpetuated the Christian error; he treated justice as only one form of obligation among others.

Coming down to our own day, we find G. E. M. Anscombe asserting, although from a quite different standpoint theoretically from Mill's, that "morally right" is not only different from but—she adds gratuitously—morally superior to "just."[2] (She immediately contradicts herself, by the way, by saying "a good man is a just man," thus conflating goodness or the disposition to do what is right with justice.) She and Mill would have been better off to stay with Aristotle's notion of "general justice" to connote the whole reach of righteousness or moral concern.

Theognis, the Greek poet of the sixth century B.C., said, "Justice contains the sum of virtues, and every just man, Kyrnos, is good." He could have reversed it by saying, "Justice contains the sum of virtues, and every good man, Kyrnos, is just." Had Anselm of Canterbury understood this, he never would have perpetrated his doctrine of atonement, according to which God's retributive justice, being at war with his merciful love, could only be satisfied by the morally outrageous death by torture on the cross of Jesus, the God-man, as an innocent substitutionary sacrifice (to wipe clean the slate of human sins).

This odious doctrine is the consequence of fragmenting the concept of obligation or duty, however unintentionally, with words like love, justice, and rightness. These represent the language of poetry in the rhetoric of ethics, but they are not substantive terms. They are only different words for the same thing, i.e., morality or moral value, and each one can serve in the place of any one of the others.

In the European heritage there is a discernible typology of the problems of justice. "Commutative" justice meant justice as between individuals—for example, in professional relations (let us say between physician and patient), or trade or business relations, or sexual and family relations, and so on. "Contributive" or legal justice included what individuals owe to the group or community, such as taxes or dues, obedience to statute or association rules, military service, school attendance, and exercise of the vote. In spite of Tittmuss's arguments, justice might support the practice in some medical centers of charging patients replacement fees for the whole blood they receive, even though it was provided free of charge in the first place by volunteer donors.[3] "Distributive" justice reversed contributive; it dealt with what the group or community owes to the individual, as in such things as social security benefits, publicly owned utilities, and health care services subsidized by the taxpayer's dollar. The fourth kind was "corporative" or social justice, as between one group or cohort and another; examples would be international relations, church and state relations, and labor-management relations.

Two things emerge clearly out of this typology. One is that justice is relational; it never arises as a problem on a desert island. The second point is that all relational actions are, in some part at least, distributive. In anything we do to others, few or many, the problem of being fair arises, and to be fair means to share benefits equitably.

In an important sense all justice is distributive, and this is because all justice (i.e., all obligation or "duty") is relational. Using St. Paul's language, our human condition is precisely that "we are members one of another." Much as we believe in religious freedom, for instance, we do not hesitate to impose inoculation on those who object to it on religious grounds, be they ever so sincere about it. Proposals to provide reasonable opportunities for sexual expression by the retarded, no matter how sincere and becoming the motive for such a proposal, could justly be limited by contraceptive sterilization in cases where the deficiency has a genetic cause.

The concept of justice has always meant in essence "rendering to each his due" (*debitum reddere*). The ethical problem is to determine what is due and, in operational terms, to whom, when, which, and how many. Ponder the distinction sometimes drawn between benevolence ("beneficence") and justice. (Sir David Ross, for one, does this.) There is an obvious difference between rendering what is due and giving more than is due, but even in a benevolent act justice is relevant as a limiting principle, for if justness is understood to be fairness, benevolence to some could be unfair if or when it injures or deprives others. Justice would not allow us to make an un-owed gift of $200 to somebody if we had reason to believe he would use it to buy a sniper rifle and shoot through his neighbor's windows. Here again we run into the canon of a fair distribution of benefits among all those affected.

If to be just means to be fair, then justice anywhere but in the Robinson Crusoe situation is essentially a matter of distribution. Put another way, what medicine calls "triage" in clinical situations is not a special form of justice; it is, rather, the very nature of justice.

The form of conscience lies in a finite world, a world of limited choices and resources.

The benefits or consequences that justice seeks are reducible to three: (1) to exclude arbitrariness, e.g., political dictatorship; (2) to ensure remedies for injuries—so-called retributive justice, as either vengeance (which is an ethically questionable version,[4] or recompense; and (3) to find a fair distribution of goods, i.e., sharing both material and immaterial values, whether in small-scale allocations like medical triage or on a bigger scale all the way up to the federal Bureau of the Budget.[5]

I think we may say that John Rawls's impact on justice thinking is greater than any philosopher's in this century. His two fundamental principles are first, as to arbitrariness, that all persons have an equal right to freedom, if compatible with the freedom of others and second, that all inequalities should be for the benefit of all and not for special interests.[6] This is reminiscent of John Stuart Mill's disapproval, and de Toqueville's, of the tendency of democratic majorities to oppress minorities. Mill said that "the only purpose for which power can be rightfully exercised over any member of a civilized community, against his will, is to prevent harm to others. His own good, either physical or moral, is not a sufficient warrant."[7] This is, of course, the principle which gives patients the right to refuse treatment. Some social thinkers also take it to justify involuntary control of human reproduction when it involves the transmission of genetic disease to the offspring.

To use a dubious phrase which ought, perhaps, to be left to the intuitionists, it seems to be practically "self-evident," as David Hume thought, that there would be no need to think about justice at all if (a) human benevolence were unlimited, and (b) if the supply of goods were not limited (and sometimes actually scarce). In short, justice is a question because of conflicts and rivalries of interest. And, as we have seen, the same can be said of ethical concern in all its forms.

As to retributive justice, prison sentences and executions are examples of vengeance rather than recompense. Many penalties in the law are of this kind. *Lex talionis*, an eye for an eye, is "getting even" with the wrongdoer, sometimes because he cannot make restitution for his unjust injury to another, sometimes in addition to or in spite of the restitution. This part of classical thinking about justice (vengeance, not restitution) is seriously called into question on ethical grounds. Walter Kaufmann has argued recently that the idea of retributive justice will soon die.[8] It is hard, certainly, to see the moral validity of feuds.

Fairness calls, of course, for restitution or recompense in cases where the injury was unmerited and the perpetrator can provide it. The issue is whether it is just (moral) to impose penalties other than restitution. A strong and common reason for "penal justice" is that it has a preventive effect. One might be inclined to think this is true, were it not for the evidence that our penal system makes beginner criminals into inveterate criminals. Nonetheless, it is surely at least reasonable to hold that not to punish crimes against persons and property invites endemic injustice.

Justice is best understood and appreciated as fair distribution, simply because we are never related to only one other individual. Commutative justice is in the last analysis an abstraction in the sense that it abstracts the patient, the client, the customer, the neighbor, or whomever it is we may be related to, from the reality of the total human community. Fairness cannot mean fair to some, not fair to others. Fairness has to be distributed. Ordinarily, for example, a physician owes confidentiality to his patient; yet he does not owe it whenever keeping a professional secret is unfair (unjust) to others— to innocent third parties. (This is why the law sometimes requires disclosures of professional secrets, under penalty of contempt of court.) A doctor could not justly remain silent if two of his or her patients were carriers of a lethal recessive gene and were proposing to marry without knowing this.

As with commutative, so with retributive justice. It is not always fair to make restitution for past injuries; you ought not to return stolen money if you know it would result in your victim's loss of his job and impoverishment of his family—as might be the case if your restitution revealed that he had let you trick him and his employer never forgave such lapses. On the other hand, when a robber recently confessed voluntarily to crimes for which a priest in Maryland had been falsely convicted, he exemplified retributive justice at its best. Obligation (justice) is always relative, and what is this but to say that it is distributive?

The Golden Rule, "Do unto others as you would have them do

unto you," is inspired by justice. Kant's categorical imperative derives from the same spirit, as does Henry Sidgwick's "axiom of justice." Kant said to act so that what you do would be normative for all, and Sidgwick said, "Whatever action any of us judges to be right for himself, he implicitly judges to be right for all other similar persons in similar circumstances."

Be it noted, however, that the relativity of justice is due as much to the variations from one person to another as to variables in different situations. There are many times when the moral agent (or, if you prefer, the just person) is faced with significantly different people, as well as circumstances. These variables always take us back to Aristotle's rule of thumb, i.e., to treat equals equally and unequals unequally (*The Laws*, book six). This is the core principle of distributive justice. Treating "unequals unequally," or as Sidgwick better expressed it, "to act dissimilarly in dissimilar cases," means that moral obligations, ought to take account of differences in persons and in circumstances.

Philosophers have neglected a disjointure between Kant's first and second maxims. The first, the universalization rule, we have already mentioned. The second was, "Treat persons as ends, not as means." But to see people as persons is to recognize their individuality and uniqueness, and this leads to difficulties with the first maxim. In dealing out justice it is easier, as the old saying goes, to be "no respecter of persons," meaning not giving persons unequal consideration. Justice is often depicted as the blindfolded goddess. But this is tantamount 'to treating persons impersonally—more as numbers than names, as objects than subjects, as entities than individuals. Thus the first and second maxims of Kant's categorical imperative run afoul of each other.

Ross, aware of the tension, spoke of moral principles (or generalized obligations) as only prima facie, meaning that ordinarily just actions may sometimes be unjust, that is to say, wrong.[9] If justice in any of its aspects is undistributed, it is in truth unfair and thus, really, unjust. In summary, we can say that justice has to be distributed because of (a) inequalities in circumstances and people, and (b) the fact that our actions are taken within the social context—i.e., that there are many, not few, who may be affected by what we do.

Aristotle's dictum that injustice occurs when equals are treated unequally and when unequals are treated equally bears reiteration. Quite frequently neither situations nor people are equal, that is to say, similar. To say, for example, that "all men are created equal" is either a piece of empty political rhetoric or actually false. It is a mistake ethically to treat generalizations about obligation, no matter how commonly they may be accepted as "fair," as if they were hard and fast moral rules. When we do this, in atypical cases we render ourselves guilty of "the immorality of morality."[10]

The complexities of just distribution are further aggravated by another problem. Which principle of selection or discrimination ought to be used as the basis of distribution? Should it be equality, or merit, or need?

Simple equalitarianism would be disastrous. As an illustration, distributing the same amount of medical care to everyone would obviously be unfair and absurd. Merit as the basis of a moral claim raises many searching questions, such as whether merit should be based on achievement, or on effort, or on worth, i.e., social function and productivity. If need were used, its criteria, whatever they were, would necessarily presuppose a standard or model condition, and what would that condition be? In a just distribution of health care, for example, what are the minimal and optimal standards of good health? And in terms of parameters, would substandard quality-of-life factors (such as the irreversible loss of cerebral function or persistent vegetative states) eliminate some patients from consideration?

Perhaps equalitarianism should be discarded as irrational, and an eclectic use of both need and merit should govern our efforts at distributive justice. As we share our goods and services—almost all of which are finite and in limited supply, if not actually scarce—only these two principles are relevant.

Occasionally we find somebody arguing that all persons are equal (born that way, or in God's eyes, or the like) and that ethically we may not choose among them or favor some over others. This is a simplistic form of equalitarianism, utterly opposed to distributive justice. Another version, but less straightforward, is to say that although we may not morally favor one person's interests over another's (e.g., their health or survival), it is all right to choose between them by chance—a flip of a coin, a roll of the dice, or pulling straws. By contrast, a consequential approach would seek to optimize or maximize the benefits to be gained by a careful distribution of available resources.

Distributive justice, whatever its principles, comes down in the end to *measurement*, to statistical adequacy, to hard numbers. At the clinical level, it would be unjust to ask a patient to decide for or against a risky operation without explaining what the statistical rate of success has been. At the administrative level, justice requires a careful measurement of the dollar costs of a whole body scanner as compared to the costs of an extramural program of diagnosis and treatment, if one has to be chosen rather than the other. Dollar costs of equipment have to be measured against potential patient loads to determine how many scanners should be acquired in a given city or population area. A good rule of thumb which all public agencies go by is that the larger the population, the more careful the measurement ("nose counts") distributive justice requires.

Another way to express this is to speak of "ethical arithmetic" or "mathematical morality." In the long run the issue between socialized medicine and private practice will hang on which policy can be shown to deliver the most health care to the most people. Under the utilitarian slogan of all liberal democracies we have to ask which policy will provide "the greatest good for the greatest number." It comes down to this: that all ethics are social ethics.

The classical medical one-to-one ethic is too fragmentary; it ignores or actually falsifies justice. Health care is a matter of moral calculus. Justice demands a telescope as well as a microscope when we look at our moral problems. To illustrate, when smokers call the prohibition of smoking in public places "health fascism," a computer analysis of the issue could go against them. Justice is a macroethical, not a microethical, problem, and the larger our population, the more justice relies on statistics.[11] Just as economics became econometrics, so ethics become ethimetrics.

How defensible is this ethical position? Half a dozen questions are ethically significant and worth further examination.

(1) If distributive justice means a fair distribution of benefits socially, does this have the effect of reducing things to the least common denominator? Does it sacrifice excellence for the sake of the aggregate good, i.e., a general participation in benefits? Could it be that democratization means mediocratization? And if so, does this

provide reason enough to put a limit on the requirements of distributive justice? If research on the artificial heart were to be abandoned because the cost of such devices would deprive too many patients of less expensive but more frequently needed treatment, would this be an example of what these objectors would have in mind—a sacrifice of top-quality cardiology for the sake of mass demand? In short, is there a conflict between excellence and distributive justice?

(2) Should *legal* justice give priority to one principle of selection over others? Should the law favor equality or need or merit? If the civil and criminal law systems are set up to be "no respecter of persons," does that mean they are equalitarian as to persons, but that "equity" allows the law to distinguish between situations and graduate its treatment accordingly—taking into account not only the "rule of necessity" (the coercion of circumstances) but factors of need and merit as well? In any event, the simplistic nature of laws often leads to revolt against them. (This is what is at stake in cases arising out of affirmative action in hiring and admission policies.)

(3) Are there some nonmoral values that are not properly subject to the justice of fair distribution? For example, music and sculpture being matters of taste, does fairness require that they be shared so as to provide an aliquot portion for everybody? To some they may be like food and drink, subjectively, but objectively they are *not* food and drink—they are not primary needs common to all. Many people would not want an equal share of either Bach or "rock," nor would they assign valid need or merit to either of them.

(4) Only a strict or consistent equalitarianism would treat all people alike. In medical triage situations, to use a dramatic illustration, it would sacrifice consequences to moralistic dogma to hold that all patients are equal and that therefore a dying or excerebrate patient has a "right" to an equal share of drugs when the supply is too meager to save both his life and a young student's. High-toned moralism (I'm going to do the 'right' thing, regardless of the consequences") is not a responsible morality and has no place in medical practice. But are there some conceivable situations, however few, in which justice could rightly choose to wear a blindfold, sticking stubbornly to the letter of a moral "law"?

(5) Since justice is relative to several variables, it follows that there are no absolute or universally obliging "rights." Justice is relative

and therefore rights are relative—both human and legal rights. Every human life is precious, but not absolutely so; it was predictable that many thousands of lives would be saved by lowering the auto speed limit to 55 miles per hour, yet it was not done until forced by the gasoline shortage. Is it possible, nonetheless, that there *are* some valid moral claims ("rights") which justice could refuse to subordinate to any counter considerations whatever? It is, of course, a commonplace in legal circles that rights are imperfect, i.e., subject to displacement—in the same way the prima facie moral duties are subject to displacement. Courts, for instance, sometimes deny mothers custody of their children in divorce and child abuse cases, and for health reasons such as the mother's mental deficiency. But are there any "moral" or "human" rights, whether established in law or not, which are always obliging? And if so, in what way would justice have to be conceptualized, in comparison or contrast to the thrust of this essay?

(6) Does "counting noses" and "reducing justice to statistics" depersonalize or dehumanize people? Is "microethics" the only genuine ethics? Pronatalists (those who oppose birth and population control), if they fear the "impersonality" of distributive justice, ought to re-examine their position—since it is precisely the lack of limits on human reproduction which directly causes massive populations and therefore, in consequence, calls for statistical distributions in order to be fair to all. Without the computer, conscience in the modern world could not function. However, those who fear that "macroethics" ignores the uniqueness of individuals are themselves ignoring the fact that social justice is multipersonal, not antipersonal. The "greatest number" is not an abstraction; it is the sum of many real, particular, and personal individuals, just as a forest is the sum of many real and particular trees.

NOTES

1. Kurt Baier, *The Moral Point of View* (Ithaca, N.Y.: Cornell University Press, 1958).

2. G. E. M. Anscombe, "Modern Moral Philosophy," *Philosophy* 33 (1958): 1-19.

3. R.M. Tittmuss, *The Gift Relationship* (London: Allen and Unwin, 1970).

4. Remember G. B. Shaw's remark, "Vengence is mine, saith the Lord. This means it is not the Lord Chief Justice's."

5. Compare this with the breakdown in Morris Ginsberg, *On Justice in Society* [London: Heinemann, 1965], pp. 51ff.

6. John Rawls, *A Theory of Justice* (Cambridge: Harvard University Press, 1971). He builds on Herbert Spencer's formula but does not cite it: "Every man is free to do what he wills provided he infringes not the equal freedom of any other man" [*Principles of Ethics*, II.46]. An American version is, "Your right to swing your fist ends where my nose begins." These maxims do not mean A has a right to smash B's nose if B is free to do the same to A. Except in an egoistic or individualistic ethics, the rule of freedom is subject to the rule of the general interest.

7. J. S. Mill, "On Liberty," *Essential Works of John Stuart Mill*, ed. Max Lerner (New York: Bantam Books, 1961), p. 263. Alexis de Tocqueville's *Democracy in America* is a standard classic.

8. Walter Kaufmann, *Without Guilt and Justice* (New York: Peter H. Whyden, 1973). He also predicts the death of retributive justice altogether, but this is because he thinks vengeance and restitution are linked like Siamese twins—which is not the case.

9. W. D. Ross, *The Right and the Good* (Oxford: Clarendon Press, 1930), pp. 16-47.

10. This delicious description of absolute rules I found in an essay of Henry Miller's, "Stand Still Like the Humming Bird" (New Directions, 1966), pp. 92-96.

11. See two papers in R. M. Veatch and R. Branson, eds., *Ethics and Health Policy* (Cambridge: Ballinger, 1976): Joseph Fletcher, "Computers and Distributive Justice" (pp. 100-109), and Clark Havighurst, "Separate Views on the Artificial Heart" (pp. 247-55).

*Hope "activates the human enterprise." Hope enables us to trans-
cend the limits of our common mortality, for hope, like feeling, em-
powers our other possibilities. Hope leads us away from despairing
acceptance of the given, "fueling the discontent that makes us resist
evil," and leads us to envision a life that is more compassionate,
just, rational, and virtuous than the one we know.*

HOPE

Kenneth Vaux

Nikos Kazantzakis, who gave us *Zorba the Greek*, had engraved on
his tombstone at Kerakleion, Crete, these words:

I HOPE FOR NOTHING . . . I FEAR NOTHING . . . I AM FREE . . .

Another epitaph guards the door at the descent into Dante's *Inferno:*

ABANDON ALL HOPE, YE WHO ENTER HERE

Here we have two understandings of the human power we call
hope. In the spirit of Marx, Freud, Nietzsche, and the artists who lust
for life, Kazantzakis asks that we revel in the concrete, the here and
now: that we not hope for anything beyond. He pities those whose
hearts are drawn away from this body, this earth, human justice.
Dante writes in a different mood. In the spirit of West Asian apocalyptic, as this world view came to shape primitive and medieval Christianity, Dante extols a transcending hope. This is hope
in God, in heaven; in salvation from existence, from suffering,
from death. Whether as a lure out of life or a saving grace within life,
both placards acknowledge that hope is a primal, vital, and moral
impulse.

The Characteristics of Hope

Hope is a virtue that activates the human enterprise, including our
response to disease and the biomedical quest. Hope gives structure
and content to our moral life by fueling the discontent that makes us

resist evil and by inspiring efforts both to endure and to ameliorate the pains of life.

To say that powers exist that make us human is to say that certain features of our life make that life unique and valuable. Persons are most fully "persons" when hope is lively. When persons are dissatisfied with what *is* because in hope they sense what *should be* or *could be*, they are authentically human.

How does hope appear in human life? In one sense it is a natural power. Since we human beings are evolving within the phylogenetic continuum of the animal world, we might expect to find the power of hope anticipated in the apes. Indeed it is. Lionel Tiger, in his recent study *Optimism: The Biology of Hope*, tells of the death of Flo, one of Jane Goodall's chimpanzees in Tanzania. The death particularly hurt Flo's son Flint. He was very close to his mother and seemed to live for her next move. He withdrew, became morose, wouldn't eat. His body slumped; he looked at the ground. He had nothing further to look forward to. He finally went to the place where he had last seen his mother's body. He was found there in a few days, dead from a normally benign virus infection. He died of suicide, of grief, of *despere*, the negation or end of hope.

Both Tiger and Edwin Wilson of Harvard have studied hope, altruism, and other human powers as these are expressed in rudimentary form in animal behavior. We are beginning to learn about hope not only from the poets and philosophers but also from the psychologists, ethologists, and endocrinologists. In the coming years some intriguing biomedical knowledge may develop as we come to understand the natural opiates, the endorphins, as these block pain and perhaps stimulate euphoria. We will also uncover more about the genetics and neurochemistry of love, anger, fear, joy, hope, and peace.

If hope is a natural power, it is also a nurtured power. It is learned. From the primitive ability of the organism to anticipate came the power in our hunter/gatherer ancestors to plan the pursuit of game. This laid down the neurological structure and provided the substratum of experience that made possible the human powers of expectancy, optimism, premonition, prediction, and hope.

We live in cultures. Cultures live by ideas, beliefs, values, and visions. As John Eccles and Karl Popper have pointed out, these noumenal features of personal and collective existence effect change in the body. Both enthusiasm and demoralization have predictable effects on the physical and mental health of people. Hope, therefore, is an instinct that is enlarged through inculcation and nurture.

But this is not the whole story. Hope has been called a theological virtue, a divine gift. In this sense it is not so much a human accomplishment as it is a divine investment. Although as physico-mental beings we are creatures of space and time, we also transcend these orders. Our life can be drawn into the supernatural and eternal realm. We can therefore speak of the biological, sociocultural, and spiritual dimensions of hope. The power is instinctive, learned, and inspired. It is a natural, nurtured, and noumenal value. How does this power, rooted in our biological nature, activated in awe and wonder, express itself in our social culture? Specifically, how does our secular hope for well-being find expression in the goals of biomedicine?

Our hope for a better life via medicine is constituted by a thousand proximate goals. These include the goals of being fertile and having children, yet being able to practice contraception; of being born free from devastating genetic disease like Tay-Sachs, sickle-cell anemia, Down's syndrome; of transacting the birth process free from trauma and disease, respiratory distress syndrome, hyaline membrane disease; of surviving childhood and youth without the lethal visitation of smallpox, polio, malaria, or failure to thrive; of achieving adulthood without the crippling effects of cancer or heart and blood-vessel disease; of securing old age without the indignities of acute and prolonged suffering. These proximate goals together comprise an unarticulated, perhaps even subconscious, human hope, the hope for release from burdens of disease, debilitation, and death: the yearning for total well-being. While these hopes may seem like the whimperings of a pampered child, we must admit that they exist with great force in our culture.

Cultural Roots of Our Hope

The biological, cultural, and moral roots of our hope have been sharpened down through history. Among others, four moments in our history, four modes of perceiving reality, have shaped our hope. Each of us living in the Western world today is (whether we know it or not) part Jew, Greek, Arab, and Christian. Each of these sources influences the way we view our experiences, the way we assign values, and the way we undertake technology. These four elements have endured in the consciousness of Western man, permeating our collective mind, activating and contouring and delimiting our hope. Without the normative impulses and boundaries conveyed in these traditions, our hope runs the danger of becoming fantasy or delusion and turning against us. It is impossible to distill the essence of these *Zeitgeiste*, these great formative periods that have shaped our mind. Yet we can isolate the salient themes as we delineate the appropriate hope in each tradition, extrapolating ethical norms from each of them in order to evaluate the stated goals of medicine today.

Matthew Arnold spoke of Israel as the people who knew the way the world was going. Yehweh is the Maker of all. He is the breath of man's life. He is the righteous judge of history. He sustains nature. He fashions space and activates time. He leads his people through suffering to the land of promise. He demands righteousness. The ideas of linear time and progress are born in this faith, as is our idea of man as steward over life and the garden of this world. The notion that the Divine Will would establish a global community where peace, justice, and health would reign is uniquely Hebrew. So is the hope that, in time, nature's anomalies—hunger, disease, war—will redemptively be healed. The important ethical derivatives of this tradition concern respect for persons, care of the earth; affirmation of an open time horizon, a passion for righteousness, and the shalom of the Lord in the earth. Our active hope that war will cease is expressed in our efforts for peace. Our active hope for a world where disease will no longer devastate people is a program of health care.

The Greeks discerned the continuities of man and nature and found them good. Man's reason is structured to understand reality. His *logistikon*, his mind, discerns the logic of nature. There are boundaries or entelechies in nature which when understood and accepted bring contentment and fulfillment. Man's noblest hope is conformation: know thyself, accept fate, honor one and all. We must stay within the given purposes of life, the *Teloi*, and not break beyond in hubris; otherwise nemesis will strike.

As classic culture collapsed, a new way of looking at the world emerged that we call apocalyptic. It began in Western Asia among those people who now live in Iran and Afghanistan. Here hope and discontent were intensified. The old order was being shaken and dismantled. A new reality was being revealed. This dawn of a new age symbolically manifested itself in nature. The earth quaked, the heavens were torn, the sick were healed, the dead were raised. In the words of the Apocalypse of the New Testament, a day will appear when there will be no tears, no pain, no death (Revelation 21:4). Apocalyptic consciousness still shapes our hope. These symbols *became* hopes and the hopes elicited tasks as Messianism was secularized. Apocalyptic hope activated two millennia of revolutions. It prompted millennial visions and utopian expectations. Here was born our mood of impatience, along with an active pursuit of a paradise vision and resistance against impediments to that vision.

Both the New Testament and the Christian church were born in the period of Jewish apocalypticism. Several elements of this new way of perceiving reality are crucial to the hope for well-being that we have inherited. The new covenant continues the anti-idolatrous or iconoclastic task of the old—of stripping the world of its demonic hold. It seeks to disenchant nature, to desacralize the world. Man can now move within and against nature without fear. The world can be perceived objectively, instrumentally, and experimentally. Here, of course, we find the roots of secularization, science, and humanism.

The hope of the Christian is gathered in a christology that sees Jesus as the Lord, the *Christokrator*. The Greek fathers, John's Gospel, Colossians, and to some extent the book of Hebrews, see the Godman as the one through whom and for whom the universe exists. The Christ-Logos is the telos, the meaning and inner direction of nature and history. Energies are now recognized within the human community, energies which are called spiritual. These new resources are seen to be healing, reconciling, integrating; they can mend brokenness. Under the influence of Greek philosophy, man is seen to be spirit, not in the Hebrew sense of being "inbreathed" but in the sense of possessing an immortal soul. This experience of a new quality of life activates an anticipation for a total regeneration and transformation of the world. This hope prompts active waiting, sometimes revolution, sometimes the lust for apocalypse, sometimes a slow and careful desire to build the earth and make a better life for people. The moral substance of the Christian hope is to care for all, especially the sick, the vulnerable, the outcast, the weak, the least of these. It seeks to overcome the demonic and diabolic, that which tortures and splits our life. It trusts in a present and coming kingdom that overwhelms the reign of pain and death.

We have inherited the legacy of Judao-Christianity, intensified by apocalypticism, contoured by Greek naturalism. How does this hope, the quest for well-being, activate the goals of modern medicine? How does this analysis of the history of moral ideas help us in a day when the energies of discovery and conquest are tempered, some say dampened, by a mood of reflection and resignation? The editor of the *New England Journal of Medicine* has written of the danger of ethics impeding medical advance. We live in a day that has seen moratoria on fetal research and DNA recombination. It is a day when a national commission seriously reflects on the ethical dimensions of behavioral and biomedical investigations, a day when the East Virginia Medical Center is authorized to make test tube babies. It is the day when Dr. Kenneth Edelin was convicted of manslaughter in Boston after aborting a fetus that some considered viable. It is a day when synagogues are stations for Tay-Sachs screening and when genetic disease is being compared to communicable disease. We have declared a war on cancer and blood-vessel disease. It is a day when Massachusetts courts decide that a dialysis patient can refuse further treatment and die. It is a day when the fear of the cost of getting sick is making people sick. It is a day when some feel they must write a living will so they may be allowed to die. In short, it is a day when the grand and noble purposes of medicine are thrown into confusion.

Hope and the Goals of Medicine

How do the goals of today's medicine grow out of the hope impulse that initially brought them into being? We can speak of four functions that medicine is being asked to perform in society.

We ask medicine to have a *preventive* function. We want to know the etiology and pathophysiology of disease. We want to know what causes sickness and how it runs its course. Where possible we want it prevented. The infectious diseases were attacked at both levels. Polio and malaria were overcome when the environmental causes were

eliminated and the preventive immunizations introduced. We are
now asking medicine, or better, the public health service, to prevent
birth defects. We will soon screen for genetic and congenital
anomalies. Parents will not knowingly bear defective children, it is
argued, nor will society allow them to if it must pay the bill. Yet even
the most basic function of medicine, *prevention*, is an ambivalent
one because we all bear morbid and lethal traits. In fact, human
creativity may be generated at least in part by these pains of existence, these "deleterious" traits.

Another function medicine performs might be called *corrective*.
Intrauterine surgery and genetic therapy remedy defects before birth.
Children are tested for PKU disease at birth and the required dietary
therapy is begun where indicated. The diabetic is treated with insu-
lin. Minor and major birth defects are surgically corrected. We attempt to excise or at least halt the spread of cancer. When the vascular
system becomes diseased, we try to reroute critical vessels or put in
synthetic ones. Much of medicine resembles maintaining a house.
The body weathers. It needs constant upkeep. Psychiatry and coun-
seling are essentially corrective medicine. The interventions are designed to restore balance, equilibrium, and function. The great majority of efforts in corrective medicine falls within the contours of the
values for well-being provoked by our hope. Questions arise only
when correcting becomes rebuilding and refashioning.

Remodeling is a third function we ask medicine to perform. Plastic
surgery for aesthetic reasons, skin tightening, bust building, or-
thodontics are major industries. These touchup jobs are not nearly as
questionable as more basic designs to make "better" people. Geneti-
cists, prompted by a value that on first reading sounds good, "that all
children have the right to be born normal" (Bently Glass), urge us to
plan mating, perhaps use nonnatural modes of fertilization and gestation, to make "better" babies. Some advocate an era of cyborg
medicine where we rebuild man with a variety of artificial parts, or-
gans, limbs. Most of us are in one way or another prosthetic people: at
least most of our mouths have been rebuilt and our eyes augmented.
Some behavior therapists hold out to us the promise of transforming
epileptic fits into controlled episodes, to turn us on from frigidity, to
transform aggression into sweetness. Some few individuals now de-
parted have not really died; they are merely "cooling it" in liquid ni-
trogen capsules until they can be cured. Curing, incidentally, is a

good word if any of you have ever eaten hickory-cured bacon. With all the positive value in this area, we might find an inordinate longing, one not appropriate to our hope, a desire we might wish to question.

The fourth purpose of medicine need not be mentioned in a civilized society. But since we do not live in such a place, we must identify this purpose. Medicine has sometimes been called on to implement societal value. At its worst it performs a retaliating or destructive purpose. A benign form of this can sneak up on us and delude us into thinking it benevolent. Several years ago a poster of a wanted criminal having a rare skin disorder was printed in a medical journal (*Archives of Dermatology*, February, 1972). "If you see this man in your office," it asked, "please inform the FBI." A few years ago the leading journal of the American Dental Association printed the record of Patty Hearst's teeth, indicating the next dental need that would bring her to the dentist's office. Fortunately, despite the patriotism of both the dermatology and dental specialties, a few have rejected the political use of their caring arts. Yet both posters were printed. One Islamic state still requires its doctors to execute the government's will to punish stealing by amputating a thief's arm.   More subtle and significant issues come when medicine is called to fulfill the malignant purposes of a state that has turned against human values. Nazi physicians practiced ktenology, the art of killing the undesirable. Some say that we have again passed the threshold of this twilight zone. Even if we have not, we need to be cautious, especially in a mass society inclined toward expediency, equipped with technological instrumentation, and possessed of a blunted conscience. We need to avoid at all costs asking the health professions to exert our values and sanctions in areas like human sexuality and anti-social behavior. We must be on guard lest the political policy of disregard for the poor continue to be expressed in our health care policy. We also need constantly to check ourselves lest we do less than the best for people because they are too old, or too small, or too sick, or too troublesome.

Tempered Hope and a More Human Medicine

We have mentioned four goals of medicine: prevention, correction, reconstruction, and retaliation. Though born in legitimate hope, each goal has inherent danger. Disaster will be averted only if the moral sensibility of each hope tradition is retained. In the light of morally tempered hope, Hebraic, apocalyptic, Greek, and Christian, what might be appropriate goals for medicine?

A constructive policy growing out of Hebraic hope would be to press with great energy into the promised future of biomedical knowledge and techniques. The age of human medicine is just beginning to dawn. We have scarcely three decades of intensive, scientifically rigorous theoretical and applied biomedicine. We can no longer afford the deviant national priorities that commit a major portion of the nation's budget to defense, espionage, and arms buildup. We are at an opportune moment in the history of medicine. Breakthroughs are possible in numerous areas. The following fields are now ready for great leaps forward: molecular biology, immunology, detection of disease, noninvasive diagnosis of disease (e.g., tomography), treatment of organic and functional brain syndromes, the development of biologicals and vaccines. We have the pool of talent. We could admit three times our present quotas of men and women to medical and graduate schools, and still be dealing with extremely gifted young people. The discouragement of misdirected science policy and the inadequate funding of research are turning the gifted youth of our society in other directions.

A mood of cynicism and romantic naturalism has set in. The cynicism over the abuses of science and the misuse of technology is well founded. We must do our research and make human applications with impeccable ethics. But the naturalism is misguided. We feel with Hippocrates that nature will take care of itself, that the body can cure itself of most ills. *Via Mediatrix Naturae*, the guild secret that the society thinks it now understands, while containing truth, is more false than true. It is not at all evident that the major ills that affect us will take care of themselves. Tumors do not regress in most cases, vascular clogging and sclerosis do not reverse themselves, genetic anomalies do not go away by themselves. We need good medicine, good research, good technology, accessible care. We've just started to claim the divine promise of healing the sick. We need to hope and act accordingly.

The Greek and especially the Stoic in us should lead us to balance exotic care with basic care for all. Heart and kidney transplants are fine if we make these available to all who need them, should the techniques prove successful in the trial population. But why should dialysis and kidney transplantation be guaranteed to all under social security when well-baby care, for example, is not? In this regard should not the national and international commitment be to a network of primary, secondary, and tertiary centers where accumulating knowledge and sensitive care provison can strengthen each other? We will very likely need incentives and imaginative use of local healers to correct present inequities.

Apocalyptic values are instructive to us as we feel and even seek for pain and suffering. Medicine should be concerned with relieving pain, not obliterating suffering. While relief of pain is a modern miracle, abolition of suffering is not a realistic or desirable goal. We are a pill-popping culture with a very low threshold for pain. We find more and more ways to anesthetize ourselves from both the signals of discord in our own bodies and the signals of pain from those around us. Our typical response to suffering, famine, war, poverty, whatever the pain may be, is either "cut it out" or turn on the television and light up another cigarette.

Suffering can be redemptive or it can be devastating, destructive of our humanity. The new drugs which are specific and local are a great benefit. But suffering will remain our lot. We must search out its meaning and its possibility. Here we need to draw on our theological heritage where normative personhood is suffering, pathetic, and empathetic, not healthy, apathetic, and independent. Looking out for number one is surely the best way to destroy ourselves.

This leads to the final suggestion. Medicine should be concerned with protecting life's possibilities rather than with fighting death. There is very likely a constant burden of morbidity that always has and always will effect the human race. Mortality is constant. If we can oversimplify the complex situation and place all human disease along a spectrum, with infectious diseases at one end, organ and degenerative disease and cancer in the middle, and mental illness at the other end, what we call medical advance may merely be pushing disease incidence around on the spectrum, increasing its incidence from one cause by decreasing it from another. Our advance on infectious and physical disease may now be pushing the disease that people most suffer over into the realm of mental illness. We may be making it harder and more painful for people to live and die. One prognosis sees two diseases as dominant in the last years of this century: AIDS and Alzheimer's. On the other hand, we may be building such pressure at that end of the spectrum that we throw disease ascendancy back to the microbes, to the plagues.

Death itself, and its symbolic prefigurations, disease, signal to man his destiny. He is condemned to die, born therefore to love and trust. Man must accept his fragmented nature as prelude to his wholeness. In the end it seems we are to live in the paradox of fighting and accepting. Perhaps a clue to this enigma is found in one of the most difficult verses in the New Testament. Paul writes to the Romans (8:20, Revised Version):

> THE CREATION WAS SUBJECTED TO FUTILITY
> NOT OF ITS OWN WILL BUT BY THE WILL OF
> HIM WHO SUBJECTED IT IN HOPE

In ancient and classic cultures the powers of being that make persons truly human were called virtues. This essay weaves together all the preceding descriptions of the singular ethical powers and sketches the general character of the moral life. Such an existence is personal, yet bound inextricably to others in community. Virtuous life is life where the powers and gifts of one and all find expression in the community. The assertive qualities of adventure and courage stimulate growth and creativity in the culture. The redeeming qualities of patience and hope allow life to proceed to grace even in the face of frustration and contradiction. Here is an answer to the questions: how shall we define and describe virtue and what bearing will this have for health, disease, and the process of care giving?

VIRTUE   Stanley Hauerwas

The Virtues: Past and Current Status

Down through the ages philosophers have seen virtue as the distinctive human quality. Classical accounts of morality, Greek as well as Christian, regarded virtue as the central concept for moral reflection. Although these accounts conflicted about what constituted virtue and which virtues should be considered primary, they agreed that consideration of morality embraced descriptions of the virtuous life.

In our time, while there is general agreement that "virtues" exist and are important, there is no consensus on how the virtues should be understood or what significance they ought to have in accounts of morality. Whether "virtue" is one or many, what the individual virtues are and which are primary, whether the virtues can conflict, how virtues are acquired and whence they issue, and whether the possession of "virtue" defines (at least in part) our humanness, are all questions on which there is little agreement. Such questions assume that "virtue" is a central concept for moral reflection—a presupposition that most current theories do not share.

For the Greeks, the term virtue, *arete*, simply meant an excellence that caused a thing to perform its function well.[1] All accounts of virtue necessarily involved some combination of excellence and power. Later Aquinas defined virtue as simply a "certain perfection of power."[2]

Therefore it is no wonder that even among those who acknowledge the significance of virtue there remains contention between theoretical and applied standards. The understanding of virtue as a moral category would seem to depend upon the controverted notion of what is entailed in "being human." Some accounts insist that the virtues are not "in" one, but "add" to our powers, thereby creating "powers," not simply perfecting potential.

Thus far there has been no satisfactory, unambiguous moral definition of the virtues. Although Plato asserted that "virtue is knowledge," the knowledge involved is not easily depicted or acquired. For Aristotle, virtues were "a characteristic involving choice, and it consists in observing the mean relative to us, a mean which is defined by a rational principle, such as a man of practical wisdom would use to determine it."[3] Aquinas accepted Aristotle's definition but spoke of a "mean between the passions."[4] Kant described that which "brings inner, rather than outer, freedom under the laws."[5] More recently, Wallace appealed for those "capacities or tendencies that suit an individual for human life generally,"[6] and Donald Evans argued that "a moral virtue is a pervasive, unifying stance which is an integral part of a person's fulfillment as a human being, and which influences his actions in each and every situation, especially his dealings with other human beings, where it helps to promote fulfillment."[7]

The very plurality of different notions of virtue indicates that any account of the virtues depends upon context. Any analysis of virtue depends upon an account of the historical nature of being human that defies all attempts to develop an ethics of virtue abstracted from society's particular traditions and history.

It is important to note that there is a significant grammatical difference between trying to define and analyze virtue and doing the same for a virtue (or the virtues). "Virtue" seems to denote a general stance of the self ("to be a person of virtue") that has remote normative significance, while "virtues" such as humility, honesty, kindness, and courage embody immediate judgments of praise. Thus many accounts of the virtues do little more than list the qualities generally praised by a society, and therefore a person who exhibits such qualities may not necessarily be a person of virtue.[8] For even

though "being a person of virtue" may be a morally ambiguous state-
ment, we can assume that the phrase "a person of virtue or character" describes a self formed in a more fundamental and substantive
manner than that possessed by other persons.

As a result, discussions of virtue or character involve analysis of
the nature of the self rather than depiction of the individual virtues.
It remains unclear, however, whether there is any necessary conceptual relation between virtue and the virtues. These concepts are no
doubt interrelated, and although discussions of virtue often treat
them as if they were the same, how they are equivalent is seldom
made explicit. This creates confusion in both critic and defender of
virtue in that what is questioned is not the significance of virtue for
the moral life but claims for the significance of specific virtues.

It is tempting to interpret the affinity between virtue and the virtues as a unity between formal and material principles. The age-old
claim that a person of virtue embodies all virtues seems, moreover,
to suggest that virtue as a formal category derives its material content from the individual virtues. This prevailing notion must be
counterbalanced by the equally significant concept that to have virtue or character involves more than a sum of the individual virtues.
Indeed, to have the virtues rightly, it was often argued, required that
one must acquire and have them as a person of character.[9]

An Ethic of Virtue

An ethic of virtue centers on the claim that an agent's being is prior
to his doing. Not that what we do is unimportant or even secondary;
rather, what a person does or does not do depends upon his possessing a "self" sufficient to take personal responsibility for his actions.[10] How persons of virtue or character act is not merely distinctive; the manner of their action must contribute to or fulfill their
moral character. This view has sometimes been misinterpreted to
imply that an emphasis on virtue encourages a justification of self-
involvement or even egoism that is antithetical to the kind of disin-
terestedness appropriate to the "moral point of view." It may be true
that an ethic of virtue does not exclude a kind of interestedness in
the self circumscribed by some Kantian interpretation of moral rationality, but attempts to designate as suspect all accounts of an

ethic of virtue as perversely self-involving or egoistic are clearly unjustified. The concern that our behavior contribute to our moral
character simply recognizes that what we do should be done in a
manner that is befitting our history as moral agents.

In this respect attempts to contrast an ethic of virtue with that of
duty are often misleading. Neither the language of duty nor that of
virtue excludes the other on principle; though often, theoretical accounts of an ethic of duty or virtue fail to describe adequately the
ways virtue and duty interrelate in our moral experience. Moreover,
while certain moral traditions seem more appropriately expressed
conceptually in terms of one rather than the other, at a formal level
there is no inherent conflict between duty and virtue. The recognition and performance of duty are made possible because we are virtuous and a person of virtue is dutiful because not to be is to be less
than virtuous.

Individuals of character have decisions or choices forced upon
them, as does anyone else. But an ethic of virtue refuses to make
such decisions the paradigmatic center of moral reflection. Morality is not primarily concerned with quandaries or hard decisions, nor is the moral self simply the collection of such decisions. As persons of character we do not confront situations as
mudpuddles into which we have to step; rather, the kind of "situations" we confront and how we understand them are a function
of the kind of people we are. Thus "training in virtue" often requires that we struggle with the moral situations which we have
"got ourselves into" in the hope that such struggle will help us
develop a character sufficient to avoid or understand differently
such situations in the future.

To be a person of virtue therefore involves acquiring the lin-
guistic, emotional, and rational skills that give us the strength to
make our decisions and our life our own. Thus individual virtues
are specific skills required to be faithful to a tradition's understanding of the moral project in which its adherents participate.
Like any skills, the virtues must be learned and coordinated in a
single life as a master craftsman has learned to blend the many
skills necessary for the exercise of any complex craft. Moreover,
such skills require constant practice, as they can simply be a
matter of routine or technique. For skills, unlike technique, give

the craftsman the ability to respond creatively to the always un-
anticipated difficulties involved in any craft in a manner that
technique can never provide. That is why the person of virtue is
also often thought of as a person of power in that his moral skills
provide him with resources to do easily what some who are less
virtuous would find difficult.

But it is also the case that the virtuous person confronts some
difficulties exactly because he is virtuous. For the virtuous life is
premised on the assumption not that we can avoid the morally
onerous but, that, rather, if we are virtuous, we can deal with the
onerous on our terms. The directive that we be virtuous necessarily challenges us to be faced with moral difficulties and obstacles that might not be present if we were less virtuous. The cow-
ard can never know the fears of the courageous. That is why an
ethic of virtue always gains its intelligibility from narratives that
place our lives within an adventure. For to be virtuous necessarily means we must take the risk of facing trouble and dangers
that might otherwise go unrecognized. The rationality of taking
such risks (with their corresponding opportunities) can only be
grounded in a narrative that makes clear that life would be less
interesting and good if such risks were absent from our lives.

From the perspective of an ethic of virtue, therefore, having
freedom is more like having power than like having a choice. For
"to have had a choice" may only mean that there were but few
options, or that one's own insufficient character limited possible
options. A virtuous person acting in freedom does not "choose"
but rather is able to claim that what was or was not done was his
own. As Frithjof Bergmann has argued,

> the making of a choice gives rise to freedom only if I identify
> with the agency that does the choosing (i.e., if I regard the
> thought-process that makes the decision as truly mine, de-
> spite its being conditioned, or influenced, or so forth), then it
> should be clear that freedom can also result from my identify-
> ing with an agency other than those processes of thought—
> and this means that I may be free even if the decisive differ-
> ence between two alternatives was not made by my choice, as
> long as I identify with (i.e. regard as *myself*) the agency that
> did tip the scales. [11]

But what allows us to claim our action as our own is the self-possession that comes from being formed by the virtues.

Some have advanced from this argument that virtuous persons could be free no matter what the circumstances—slavery, rack or the throne. There is a sense in which this may be true, though it is probably wrongly put, for the question is not whether they are "free" but whether they have ceased to be virtuous. Nevertheless, one cannot therefore assume that an ethic of virtue is therefore indifferent to social circumstance. Rather, our capacity to be virtuous depends upon the existence of communities that have been formed by narratives faithful to the character of reality.

The connection between freedom and self-possession in the virtuous person points to the centrality of the agent for an ethic of virtue. For the subject of virtue can be none other than the self, which has its being only as an agent with particular gifts, experiences, and history. Thus persons of virtue or character are often described as "their own man"; similarly, possessing "character" means "being a person of integrity." By definition, integrity denotes the courage to "march to a different drummer."

While we may admire such persons, we assume that a full ethical life demands more than integrity. After all, Gordon Liddy seems to have had integrity of a sort; persons of integrity sometimes commit extreme deeds in the interest of preserving their fortitude or remaining faithful to a given creed. Because of this possible equation of integrity with consistency, many must assume that the very meaning of morality necessitates the qualification of our agency by a more universal or disinterested point of view. In such a view the moral life would be lived (as an ethic of virtue seems to imply) from the perspective not of the artist but of the art-critic.

While no doubt judges and disinterested observers have characteristics appropriate to such stances, they cannot be those necessary for a person of virtue. For it is morally necessary, if one is to have character or to be a person of virtue, that it be one's *own* character. Therefore, an ethic of virtue seems to entail a refusal to ignore the status of the agent's "subjectivity" for moral formation and behavior. Even as integrity requires that one be faithful to personal history, so the development of a person of virtue mandates being faithful to a community's history. Exactly because an ethic of virtue

has such a stake in the agent's perspective, it is profoundly committed to the existence of communities convinced that their future depends on the development of and trust in persons of virtue.

The Politics of Ethics and the Neglect of Virtue

Despite the recent interest in the ethics of character and virtue,[12] it is
generally conceded that modern moral philosophy has neglected the
virtues.[13] Much of this neglect can be attributed to the concern of
moral philosophers to expurgate and deny status to the "subjective"
in moral argument and justification. Many assume that giving cre-
dence to the subject in the manner an ethic of virtue seems to involve would prevent us from demonstrating how relativism (and
perhaps even egoism) are morally untenable. Some contend that the
defeat of relativism and egoism is the great project and task of modern ethics. Yet the reason for neglecting the subject is more revealing. It may have originated in a tacit fear that we lack the kind of
community necessary to sustain development of people of virtue
and character.[14] It is not primarily an issue of ethical theory, then,
but of politics. That is, contemporary ethicists are attempting an
account of the moral life while avoiding the necessary risks con-
comitant to all significant attempts at community and corresponding ethics of virtue.

Such claims may appear far too dramatic, as it can be objected that
there are some quite plausible and more mundane reasons for the
neglect of virtue incontemporary moral discussion. It is often
pointed out that there is hardly any way to portray "the virtuous person" or the "person of character" without reference to some antecedent criteria of good or right. Thus concepts of virtue are parasitic
upon prior concepts of good or duty. That is why, in spite of deep disagreements, both teleologist and deontologist assume that questions
of the nature of virtue are secondary to genuine ethical issues.

This presumption is often reinforced by the commonplace assumption that a person's moral character can be analyzed by determining the worth of both his actions and his intentions. In this view,
"matters of moral character seem not only dependent upon but
exhaustively definable in the language of act morality."[15] Many
argue, therefore, that an ethics of virtue depends first upon an ac-

count of what acts should or should not be done: only when such an account were compiled would we have a basis for knowing what kind of virtues we ought to have.

Hence Frankena delineates three primary theories of virtue necessarily dependent upon prior theories of normative ethics i.e., trait-egoism, trait-utilitarianism, and trait-deontological theories. Frankena defends the form of the latter, pointing out that "an ethics of duty or principles also has an important place for the virtues." For "principles without traits are impotent and traits without principles are blind." While important to ensure that we know what we *should* do, Frankena contends against anyone advocating an ethic which says it is not the function of virtue to tell us *what* to do. For that we must rely upon the two deontic principles, beneficence and equal treatment, plus "the necessary clarity of thought and factual knowledge."[16]

Utilitarians are often even less interested in the agent and the virtues than are the many kinds of deontologists. Thus R. M. Hare has argued:

> It is important to distinguish between judgments about the moral rightness of an act and those about the moral worth of the agent . . . .
> Utilitarianism . . . has seldom been advocated primarily as a way of judging agents. If it is so used, it will have to pay as much attention to motives and intentions as any other theory. Good motives and intentions will be benevolent ones, arising from the desire to do what is best for the people affected by our acts. As we shall see this may engender a respect (because of the good which comes therefrom) for the moral principles which anti-utilitarians too revere. But utilitarians have generally been less interested in the question "Will this act put me in the category of good or of sinful men?" than in the question "Ought I now to do this Act? Would it be the right thing to do?" and they have said that we must answer this question by examining the consequences.[17]

Proponents of an ethic of virtue would not deny that every society rightly singles out certain forms of behavior which it prohibits or recommends irrespective of the character or intentions of the agents. Yet this "fact" is not sufficient to establish the further claim that the rightness or wrongness of any behavior, whether teleologically or deontologically justified, is logically prior to an account of virtue. The assumption of such priority necessarily distorts our moral psychology. For we as agents know that our actions (both what we have done and what we have not done) seldom provide adequate indications of our moral worth. Assessment of one another solely on the basis of our actions does not adequately describe ourselves (though often what we do may well be a crucial test case to show that our assumptions about what we "really are" are not in fact congruent with what we are). Rather, we wish to be judged by the way our "actions" gain their intelligibility as they are understood in the context of our history, our character.

Lawrence Becker has suggested that self-esteem is often the crux in evaluations of our own conduct:

> . . . self-esteem is not built entirely on estimates of the value or dutifulness of one's performance. No matter how many successes some people have they still feel like they are failures; no matter how many lies some people tell, they still feel they "are" fundamentally honest. Moral theorizing which ignores or slights this—as act theory tends to do—is very often beside the point in concrete moral situations.[18]

Moreover, self-esteem, and subsequent respect for others, seem to involve the willingness to accept responsibility not just for acts but for ourselves as "having a self-reality that is always both to be discovered and recognized on the one hand and further constituted and determined on the other."[19] The essence of such self-esteem depends on our having the self-constitutive ability to conceive and live it—i.e., the very power commensurate with being a person of virtue or character.

Recognizing the significance of virtue does not imply that questions of performance or behavior are irrelevent for moral evaluations. It is certainly appropriate, especially in legal contexts, for a society to single out certain kinds of behavior which are excluded, irrespective of the agent's interests. Yet perhaps such "abstractions" gain their rationale in reminding us not merely what our conduct should and should not be, but what *we* should be. Thus it could be that common prohibitions, such as that against murder, also function to remind us that we should be people who respect the life of another.

Moreover, evaluations of "acts" are crucial for the growth of our own character and virtue. For it is through descriptions of our behavior tested against other accounts that we check ourselves against self-deception and self-righteousness.[20] Nevertheless, the truthfulness of such reports cannot be ensured as the result of being formed allegedly from "the moral point of view," but rather depends upon their representing the wisdom of virtuous persons from a community's past and present.

Current theories of normative ethics, in concentrating on acts[21] prior to any account of virtue, are problematic, since they miss something we think vital to the moral life. Indeed, prescriptions of moral justification of conduct from the "moral point of view" may have appeared intelligible only in that we continued to expect that people would be trained to be virtuous in the future. The difficulty, however, is that such theories cannot supply and perhaps even tend to impede considerations crucial to the development of such people.

The focus on acts, as Lawrence Becker has reminded us, cannot explain why

> there are people whose performance is consistently good—even saintly—who seem untouched by ignoble purposes to the degree we have come to expect in our fellows, and whom we still will not call, in any unreserved sense, "good people." We will not so describe them when we think that their virtue is simply blind adherence to authority training, for example—or, as one of Steinbeck's characters, merely due to lack of energy. Similarly, there are people whose performance is consistently bad—even malevolent—but who exhibit not just remorse after the fact, and surely not just regret, rather a tragically accurate self-perception which makes us unable to call them, in any unreserved sense, "bad people."[22]

No theory of "moral rationality" or the "moral point of view" can in itself supply an account sufficient to explain why we think such judgments appropriate. Rather, what is required is an appreciation of why significant depictions of morality presuppose and require the existence of societies who know that their moral life relies on the vitality of persons of character and virtue.

Contemporary discussions of morality which neglect or, at any rate, make virtue secondary, attempt to develop an ethical theory which is not founded on such a moral community. Morally and politically, we act as though we are members of no community, share no goods, and have no common history. Thus the challenge for contemporary ethical theory is to provide a theory of how moral "objectivity" can be achieved in such a society. By providing an impersonal interpretation of "moral rationality" in which the emotions and history of the agent are relegated to the "private," recent moral theory has tried to show how moral argument (and even agreement) is possible between people who otherwise share nothing in common. It is thought "morality" can be grounded in human nature; only now "nature" is limited to "rationality," abstracted from any particular community's history.

Rather than condemn contemporary moral theory for being trivial and/or abstractly irrelevant, it must be seen as an extraordinary moral project which seeks to secure societal cooperation between moral strangers short of reliance on violence.[23] Such an endeavor should not be lightly criticized or dismissed. But neither can it be accepted, since its failure to properly account for the moral agent distorts our nature. In the interest of securing tolerance between different people we are forced to pay the price of having our differences rendered morally irrelevant, for recognition of such differences provides the basis for fear and envy. As a result our nature, as we are agents in and of history, is obscured.

Only from the perspective of an ethic that attempts to free morality from history would an ethic of virtue look like a subjectivistic threat to morality. While an ethic of virtue is certainly an agent morality, virtue does not thereby denote a private morality in contrast with a more fundamental and important public morality. Indeed, the very distinction between public and private, social and individual morality is a theory-dependent distinction that is antithetical to an ethic of virtue.[24] An ethic of virtue necessarily involves an account of how every polity, implicitly or explicitly, entails a narrative which depicts what a person of character should be as well as how certain virtues, in their interrelation, are central to the moral life. But even more strongly, we must see how polity is ultimately tested by the kind of people it develops.

In this sense, then, there can be no theory of virtue, for any such is necessarily relative to the history of a particular community. All renderings of the virtues, therefore, imply—implicitly or explicitly—an understanding of human nature and history.

The Virtues and Human Nature

The most striking indication of the historical nature of virtue must be the diversity of virtues recommended by different societies and thinkers. Indeed, one of the things that must make attention to the virtues so unappealing is the lack of consensus about which virtues are morally central and, perhaps even more frustrating, the absence of any principle or method to determine what the primary virtues are or how they might be interrelated. It is no wonder that one is tempted to abandon all interest in the virtues for the less messy and seemingly more fundamental task of providing a rational foundation for morality.

Certainly, no agreement exists about which virtues should be considered central. Plato, for example, emphasized in the *Republic* courage, temperance, wisdom, and justice,[25] central virtues because he interpreted them as crucial for functions necessary in the Republic. However, he also suggested that these fulfilled or perfected various aspects of the soul.

Even though Plato's account of the virtues has often been criticized because of what many take to be his faulty psychology, such criticism fails to touch the significant insight contained in his argument. For Plato rightly suggested that any analysis of the virtues requires some account of how they are necessary for the fulfillment of our nature and for the working of the good society. When the virtues are simply treated as "excellences" for the fulfillment of our human nature, divorced from any political context, they cannot help but appear arbitrary. But of course that is exactly what happpened as the increasing disintegration of Greek society made implausible the political significance of the virtues. As a result, it became necessary to show that particular virtues gained their meaning and intelligibility as forms of fulfillment of particular aspects of human nature.

Such strategy was doomed to fail. As Aristotle argued, our nature does not dictate what the virtues should be; instead, they "are implanted in us neither by nature nor contrary to nature: we are by nature equipped with the ability to receive them, and habit brings this ability to completion and fulfillment."[26] No less insistent than Plato that ethics was but a branch of politics, unlike Plato, Aristotle made no attempt to establish any list of central virtues. Struck by the diversity of constitutions and considering it impossible to provide any one account of the ideal state with a corresponding set of virtues, Aristotle was forced to rely on the clumsy device of the mean in order to compile what is almost a grocery list of virtues. Courage, self-control, generosity, magnificence, high-mindedness, gentleness, friendliness, truthfulness, wittiness, justice, and even a nameless virtue that was a mean between ambition and lack of ambition are those qualities which he deemed characteristic of the Greek gentleman.

In Christian theology accounts of the virtues were even less systematic. Listed among the "fruits of the Spirit" by St. Paul were love, joy, peace, patience, kindness, goodness, faithfulness, gentleness, and self-control (Galatians 5:22-23). Christians, especially in the early centuries, made no attempt to establish any one list of the virtues or to show why certain virtues were more fundamental or more grounded in our nature. Indeed, the Christian appropriations of the concept of virtue introduced some difficulty. Augustine argued that in a significant sense virtue cannot be based upon or be a possession of the soul. Rather, as a gift of God "either virtue exists beyond the soul, or if we are not allowed to give the name of virtue except to the habit and disposition of the wise soul, which can exist only in the soul, we must allow that the soul follows after something else in order that virtue may be produced in itself."[27] Unless this "something else" is God, the virtues are but forms of self-love and become nothing more than glorious vices. The fourfold division of virtue in Augustine's writings must be understood as four forms of love:

> Temperance is love giving itself entirely to that which is loved; fortitude is love readily bearing all things for the sake of the loved object; justice is love serving only the loved object, and therefore ruling rightly; prudence is love distinguishing with sagacity between what hinders it and what helps it. The object of this love is not anything, but only God, the chief good, the highest wisdom, the perfect harmony.[28]

Aquinas in many ways culminated the reflection on virtue, as his compilation combined the influence of Plato, Aristotle, the Stoics,[29] and Augustine in an extraordinarily complex manner. Though his account of the nature of the virtues as habits and how we acquire them primarily depended upon Aristotle, he attempted to correlate the individual cardinal virtues with functions of the soul. Just as temperance directs and fulfils the concupiscible and courage the irascible passions, prudence perfects the practical intelligence and justice guides all our "operations."[30] The simplicity of this scheme, however, betrays the complexity of Aquinas's account. He was well aware that a "diversity of objects" could cause a "diversity of passions without causing diversity of virtues, as when one virtue is about several passions"; or a diversity of objects "from causing different virtues without causing a difference of passions, since several virtues are directed towards one passions, for example, pleasure."[31] Moreover, following Augustine, Aquinas maintained that the theological virtues of faith, hope, and charity must be infused in us if the "natural virtues" are to be properly formed and directed.

Even if it were possible to compile a list of virtues common to all philosophical systems, this would not demonstrate that there is a unique set of virtues required by our common human nature. Although there might be widespread consensus on the importance of such virtues as temperance and courage, agreement often extends no further than the name. As soon as the question of substance is raised, sharp disagreements appear as to what courage or temperance entail. For the meaning of courage and temperance varies depending upon what society considers paradigmatic examples of temperance or courage.

The diversity of the meaning and kinds of virtues does not imply, however, that all attempts to depict the virtues are arbitrary. Rather than revealing that there is no human nature, this diversity reveals the historical nature of our human existence that requires and makes intelligible the individual and social necessity of the virtues for the moral life. As humans we cannot be anything we wish, but our nature demands that we wish to be more than our nature. As Aristotle and Aquinas suggested, it is through our habits that we acquire a "second nature," and so far as those habits are virtuous they furnish us with a nature befitting our moral stature.

Some, dissatisfied with the "looseness" of such accounts, have sought to depict human nature as sufficient to show why one set of virtues, or at least why certain virtues, must be preferred over all others. This often involves the claim that there is a distinctive aspect of being human that distinguishes us from all other species— i.e., rationality. However, as Mary Midgley has argued, what is special about each creature, including humans,

> "is not a single, unique quality but a rich and complex arrangement of powers and qualities, some of which it will certainly share with its neighbors. And the more complex the species, the more true this is. To expect a single differentia is absurd. And it is not even effectively flattering to the species, since it obscures our truly characteristic richness and versatility."[32]

Perhaps more troubling, when rationality is claimed as our distinctive nature, undue emphasis is placed upon intellect as the sole source and basis of virtue. To be sure, there are powerful and profound reasons for this, as Aquinas was certainly right to claim that moral virtue cannot obtain without prudence.[33] Moreover, since the human condition involves many activities which often seem without coherence, it is only with our "Minds" that we exert order in our lives at all. Thus reason has been conjectured as the basis for our historicity because it alone gives the power to act.

However, as Bernard Williams has suggested, claims of rationality as the distinguishing mark of man tend "to acquire a Manichean leaning and emphasize virtues of rational self-control at the expense of all else."[34] Indeed, when reason is made the primary source and basis of the virtues, their very substance is distorted, for then they appear to be the means to control our nature and passions. But as Aristotle and Aquinas insisted, the virtues are a unique blend of "nature" and "reason," since our passions need not so much control as direction. Thus Aquinas argued that only because the Stoics mistakenly understood passion as any affection in discord with reason did they argue that virtuousness required the suppression or eradication of all passion.[35] Once passions are correctly understood as "movements of the sensitive appetite," not only are they allowed in a virtuous man, but the virtuous man cannot be without them.

What must be rejected is what Robert Solomon has called the "myth of the passions" that interprets the passions as the antithesis to "reason." On the basis of this myth the passions are seen as animal intrusions and physiological disruptions that reason must control.[36] In contrast to the myth, Solomon argues that the passions are our

> self-esteeming representations of emotions as our own judgments, with which we structure the world to our purposes, carve out a universe in our own terms, measure the facts of reality, and ultimately "constitute" not only our world but ourselves. Rather than disturbances or intrusions, these emotions, and the passions in general, are the very core of our existence, the system of meanings and values within which our lives either develop and grow or starve and stagnate.[37]

The passion of reason and the reason of the passions involved in any account of virtue is an indication of our historical nature.[38] Just as history cannot be separated from the natural, as nature is the very stuff of history, neither can reason be separated from the passions. Being human means our reason and our passions find their fulfillment in and through the virtues. Put more strongly, it is a mistake to argue whether reason or passion is more basic to human nature, since those aspects of the self are intelligible and are shaped through the virtues. The only way to be human is to be habitual—which is to say, historical.

Indeed, the virtues are the prerequisites illuminating our history as destiny rather than fate. The power of virtue provides the self-possession necessary to avoid the parameters of life that others would impose. That virtue provides such power is the basis for the axiom that virtue is "its own reward," though such a claim does not mean that the virtues offer no benefit. The phrase "virtue is its own reward" reminds us that choosing to be virtuous can be for no reason other than that to be so is the only condition under which we would desire to survive. Only by so embodying the virtues have we the power to make our lives our own.

The Virtues and the Histories of Our Communities

This analysis of the nature and significance of virtue should enable us to understand today's peculiar moral situation. For if, as argued, an ethic of virtue depends upon a particularly strong claim and commitment to the historical nature of human existence, and if the specification of individual virtues and their relation derives from the traditions of a particular community, then we develop some inkling why many currently feel so morally lost. As individuals we express a lack of common history or community sufficient to provide us with the resources necessary for us to make our lives our own. Yet our problem is not that we have inherited an oppressive history, or that we exist in coercive societies, but that we inherit too many histories and participate in too many communities, each with its own account of what constitutes being virtuous.[39]

Fortunately no society is so well ordered that all moral conflicts are excluded. Every substantive tradition generates diverse interpretations that give rise to conflict. In our current situation we lack any schema for resolving such conflict societally and, even more significantly, internally. Bereft of virtues sufficient to structure either self-esteem or self-possession, in the absence of the faculties that are developed only through virtue, we employ forms of power and violence which seem to guarantee our only security.[40]

The plurality of communities, moreover, helps to explain the peculiar moral power of the traditional professions. If every polity derives from a corresponding training in virtue, the professions must be regarded as some of the few remaining coherent polities. That is why, despite their claims of moral neutrality, medical and law schools survive as our closest modern analogs to ancient schools of virtue. In the commitment to their clients' welfare through the practice of developed skills, they exemplify a training in virtue from which they derive profound self-esteem. That is why their profession becomes the source of identity and justification, as occupation is one of the few areas in life which leads itself to exposition. The attempt of many unskilled to claim professional status, perhaps seeking to trade upon the prestige of the traditional professions, can be interpreted as grasping for moral coherence.

Moral coherence, however, cannot be supplied even by the professions. Not only are their traditional commitments increasingly qualified by our moral pluralism, but no one can live morally as a professional only. All effort to deal with human existence as a "lawyer" or "doctor" cannot succeed. The virtues and skills of the professions were not, nor can they ever be, sufficient to negotiate the moral demands our lives inevitably place upon us.

Because we find ourselves always involved in intricate webs of conflicting relationships and duties, it is imperative that the ultimate guide must issue from personal resources. Authenticity thereby is signaled as the hallmark of our morality, through which we can initiate the "downward movement through all the cultural superstructures to some place where all movement ends."[41] Conscience thus becomes the ultimate authority for our behavior.

Yet the function of conscience, David Little has observed, works only in a peculiar relation to the possessor of conscience, to our identity as self. The very notion of conscience involves the "business of sustaining the identity and continuity, of protecting the integrity of the person as actor, at the deepest levels of the self."[42] But if the primary task of conscience is to sustain the achievement through time of personal identity and integrity, it seems to require some combination of virtues such as wisdom, courage, honesty, temperance. Perhaps that is why many in the past have said that the duty to be a person of conscience is not just a personal necessity but a social responsibility.[43] If conscience requires some account of the virtues, then appeal to it as a court of last resort is more a symptom of our moral situation than its solution.[44] That may be the reason so many today rely on cynicism to sustain the self. When the presuppositions necessary to uphold a society's ethic of honor are no longer tenable, cynicism becomes morally indispensable.[45] Through our cynicism—that is, the rigorous and disciplined attempt to investigate the self-interest behind every moral claim—we seek to avoid the loss of the self by denying overriding loyalty to any one cause or community or disintegration among the many.

Yet in the process is lost the very soil crucial to the growth of virtue—the self-esteem cultivated by the sense of sharing a worthy adventure. For a rigorous cynicism is too powerful. Even as we call into question the moral commitments of others, we cannot save ourselves from its destructive gaze. Cynicism leaves us only with the consolation that because we recognize our own deception we are not hypocrites or fools. Of course, there is no deeper deceit than the assumption that we are among those free from deception.

Moreover, cynicism cannot sustain itself, as it is too easily captured by powers it does not have the means to name, much less avoid. As historical beings we cannot avoid living someone's history even if we think our cynicism has freed us from all commitments.

We are not free from all narratives, nor can we choose any story. Our only escape from destructive histories, having the virtues trained by a truthful story, can come solely through participation is a society that claims our lives in a more fundamental fashion than any profession or state has the right to do.

Only through such a society do we have the possibility of acquiring those virtues capable of countering cynicism—hope and patience. For the virtuous life is inherently adventurous as people of virtue claim, in spite of all evidence to the contrary that our existence is responsive to moral endeavor. We are thus sustained by hope that the adventure of living virtuously will be worth the risk. Hope thus forms every virture, for without hope the virtuous cannot help but be ruled by despair.

But hope without patience results only in the illusion of optimism or, more terrifying, the desperation of fanaticism. The hope necessary to initiate us into the adventure must be schooled by patience if the adventure is to be sustained. It is through patience that we learn to continue to hope, even though our hope seems to offer little chance of fulfillment. Patience is training in how to wait when there seems no way to resolve our moral conflicts or even when we see no clear way to go on.[46] Patience is able to wait because it is fueled by the conviction that our moral projects, and in particular the central moral project we call the self, will prevail. Yet patience equally requires hope; without hope patience too easily accepts the world and the self for what it is rather than what it can or should be.

Only by hope and patience, therefore, are we able to sustain a self capable of withstanding the disintegration that is threatened by the necessity of recognizing the inescapable plurality and often unresolved nature of our moral existence. We do not live in a world that is capable of being negotiated by one virtue, but neither can we live without a self formed by the hope and patience sufficient to make our life our own. Without hope we lack the resource even to have a self befitting our moral nature, but without patience we lack the skills for the self to acquire a history sufficient to be a self.

Without denying that there may be nonreligious accounts of hope and patience, Jews and Christians have been the people who have stressed the particular importance of these virtues. For they are the people formed by the conviction that our existence is bounded by a power that is good and faithful. Moreover, they are peoples with a deep stake in history, as they believe God has charged them with the task of witnessing to his providential care of our existence. They therefore believe their history is nothing less than the story of God's salvation of them and all people. Such a history does not promise to make the life of virtue easier or our existence safer. Rather, such a story, with its corresponding society, offers training in the hope and patience necessary to live amid the diversity of the world, trusting that its very plurality reflects the richness of God's creation and redeeming purpose.

Whether hope and patience can be sustained in a world and a society like ours that no longer thinks such trust is warranted remains to be seen. It is not that in the absence of God people lack the resources to live morally. People will usually find the means to live decently. Rather, a more profound question arises: whether in the absence of God people can find the resources, socially and personally, to form and sustain the virtues necessary to recognize and fulfill our historical nature.[47]

NOTES

1. Werner Jaeger's *Paideia*, Vols. 1-3 (Oxford: Basil Blackwell, 1939), still remains the classical treatment of the meaning of *arete* in Greek culture; see particularly 1:3-14.) For a brief account see C. B. Kerferd, "Arete," *Encyclopedia of Philosophy*, Vol. 1, ed. Paul Edwards (New York: Free Press, 1967), pp. 147-48.

2. Thomas Aquinas, *Summa theologica*, I-II, 55, 1, tr. Fathers of the English Dominican (Chicago: Encyclopedia Brittanica, 1952).

3. *Nichomachean Ethics*, tr. Martin Ostwald (New York: Bobbs-Merrill, 1962), 1106b35-37.

4. Aquinas, *Summa theologica*, I-II, 59, 1-2.

5. Immanuel Kant, *The Doctrine of Virtue*, tr. Mary Gregor (New York: Harper Torchbooks, 1964), p. 380.

6. James Wallace, *Virtures and Vices* (Ithaca, N.Y.: Cornell University Press, 1978), p. 37. Philippa Foot suggests "that virtues are in general beneficial characteristics, and indeed ones that a human being needs to have for his own sake and that of his fellows." See *Virtues and Vices and Other Essays in Moral Philosophy* (Berkeley: University of California Press, 1976), p. 3.

7. *Struggle and Fulfillment* (New York: Collins, 1979), p. 14.

8. The novels of Jane Austen are studies in the difficulty of distinguishing persons of character from those who simply exhibit virtues in a polite society. It was Austen's great insight that "the person of character" is not necessarily at odds with societal manners but often the person for who manners are second nature. Convention may well stifle moral growth, but it may also be the condition necessary for becoming virtuous. Yet that very condition also often makes difficult our ability to distinguish a person of character from those that are but observers of convention.

9. Aristotle and Aquinas both maintained that only those virtues acquired in a manner befitting a person of virtue can be said to "be" virtuous. (See Aristotle, *Nichomachean Ethics*, 1105a30-1105b8, and Aquinas, *Summa theologica*, I-II, 65, 1.) For analysis of the problem of circularity in Aristotle's and Aquinas's accounts of the virtues, see my "Character, Narrative, and Growth in the Christian Life," forthcoming.

10. While contemporary philosophical ethics bases the ability to claim our action as our own in the "autonomy" of the self, I suggest that the self is formed by tradition and its correlative virtues, sufficient to interpret our behavior truthfully.

11. *On Being Free* (South Bend, Ind.: Notre Dame Press, 1977), p. 65.

12. See, for example, the work of James Gustafson, Alasdair MacIntyre, Elizabeth Anscombe, Stuart Hampshire, Philippa Foot, and the works cited earlier.

13. Peter Geach alleges that philosophy has overlooked the virtues in his *The Virtues* (Cambridge: Cambridge University Press, 1977).

14. For example, Alasdair MacIntyre has argued that much of the work in contemporary English and American moral philosophy is more a symptom than a cure for the disease it takes as its object to eradicate. See "Why Is the Search for the Foundations of Ethics So Frustrating?" *Hastings Center Report* 9, 4 (Aug. 1979): 20.

15. Lawrence C. Becker, "The Neglect of Virtue," *Ethics* 85, 2 (Jan., 1975): 111.

16. See William Frankena, *Ethics* (Englewood Cliffs, N.J.: Prentice-Hall, 1973), pp. 65-67. For a more extended treatment of Frankena's positon, see my "Obligation and Virtue Once More" and Frankena's response, "Conversation with Carney and Hauerwas" in *Journal of Religious Ethics* 3, 1 (1975): 27-67. See also my *Truthfulness and Tragedy* (South Bend, Ind.: Notre Dame Press, 1977), pp. 40-56.

17. "Utilitarianism," *Encyclopedia of Bioethics*, ed. Warren Reich (New York: Free Press, 1978), p. 425. See also Bernard Williams, "A Critique of Utilitarianism," in *Utilitarianism: For and Against* (Cambridge: Cambridge University Press, 1973), p. 116.

18. Becker, "Neglect of Virtue," p. 112.

19. Alan Montefiore, "Self-Reality, Self-Respect, and Respect for Others," *Midwest Studies in Philosophy*, 3 (Morris: University of Minnesota, 1978): 201. One of the deepest moral issues for any community is how to preserve

the necessary differences between individuals without injustice and envy corrupting all grounds for moral cooperation.

20. See my *Truthfulness and Tragedy*, pp. 82-100.

21. Not only do such theories fail to account for the significance of virtue, but they equally ignore the problem of defining and interpreting moral behavior. It is almost as if they assumed that a description (such as that of abortion) is simply there to be seen rather than being the creation of a particular community's experiences and history. See my *Vision and Virtue* (South Bend, Ind.: Fides/Claretian, 1974), pp. 11-29, 127-65.

22. Becker, "Neglect of Virtue," p. 113. Perhaps these ambiguities explain why those who wrestle with descriptions of the moral life in the language of virtue have frequently been attracted to the psychoanalytic process as a paradigm of moral reflection.

23. See, for example, W. B. Gallie's analysis of Kant's commitment to peace in *Philosophers of Peace and War* (Cambridge: Cambridge University Press, 1978), pp. 8-36.

24. Ed Long, in his "The Social Roles of the Moral Self," in *Private and Public Ethics*, ed. Donald Jones (New York: Edwin Mellen Press, 1978), argues that virtues necessarily imply public and social commitment (pp. 158-79); see also the essays in *Public and Private Morality*, ed. Stuart Hampshire (Cambridge: Cambridge University Press, 1978..

25. Tr. F. D. Cornford (New York: Oxford, 1964), pp. 119-44.

26. Aristotle, *Nichomachean Ethics*, 1103a23-25. Cf. my *Character and the Christian Life* (San Antonio, Tex.: Trinity University Press, 1975), pp. 45-60, and "Character, Narrative, and Growth in the Christian Life."

27. "On the Morals of the Catholic Church," in *Christian Ethics: Sources of the Living Tradition*, ed. Waldo Beach and H. R. Niebuhr (New York: Ronald Press, 1955), p. 112. Centures later Niebuhr argued that the concept of virtue is alien to Christian morality as the latter is a gift rather than an achievement or the product of training. See "Reflections on Faith, Hope and Love," *Journal of Religious Ethics* 2, 1 (1974): 152.

28. Augustine, "Morals of the Catholic Church," p. 115.

29. I have not indicated the nature of Stoic thought on the virtues as it seems to me from a theoretical perspective largely in grouping under the names of the virtues certain public duties. Aquinas followed the Stoic example in Vols. I-II of his *Summa*, and it was that aspect of his work that became central for later Roman Catholic ethics. Thus the language of the virtues remained though they were interpreted primarily as duties to be performed.

30. Ibid., 69, 4. Justice, unlike the other virtues, does not form a passion so much as provide force deficient of motivation. See, for example, Philippa Foot's interesting remarks on this in her *Virtues and Vices*, pp. 9-11.

31. Aquinas, *Summa theologica*, 60, 4.

32. *Beast and Man: The Roots of Human Nature* (Ithaca, N.Y.: Cornell University Press, 1978), p. 207.

33. Yet Aquinas insisted also that prudence could not operate without the

other virtues. For discussion of this see Josef Pieper, *The Four Cardinal Virtues* (South Bend, Ind.: Notre Dame Press, 1966), pp. 3-42.

34. *Morality: An Introduction to Ethics* (New York: Harper Torchbooks, 1972), pp. 65-66.

35. Aquinas, *Summa theologica*, I-II, 59, 2.

36. *The Passions* (Garden City: Anchor Press, 1976), pp. 15, 187. Cf. Solomon's analysis of the passions (pp. 186-93) with Evans's account of the attitudes in his *Struggle and Fulfillment* (pp. 12-13).

37. Solomon, *The Passions*, p. xvii. Although I find Solomon's analysis of the passions compelling, I think his attempt to ground morality in the passions is but the other side of the Kantian attempt to ground morality in reason. Both seek to avoid a particular society's history as the locus of moral development and reflection.

38. But see Dr. Patricia Jung's Vanderbilt dissertation, "The Embodied Nature of Character: A Study in Theological Ethics" (1979) for a contrasting account of character.

39. MacIntyre has developed this theme in a number of his recent articles. For the fullest account see his *A Short History of Ethics* (New York: Macmillan, 1966).

40. That is why all genuine forms of nonviolence require such extraordinary forms of training in virtue. Only those who are people of power can risk denying themselves the protections most of us feel we need if we are to survive psychologically and physically. Moreover, the nonviolent need not only to be virtuous but to participate in a community that provides them with the moral resources for living nonviolently. The disadvantages correlative to living nonviolently can quickly generate self-hate if we are not sustained by a more substantive community that is able to remind us what we are about.

41. Lionel Trilling, *Sincerity and Authenticity* (Cambridge, Mass.: Harvard University Press, 1972), p. 12.

42. "Duties of Station vs. Duties of Conscience: Are There Two Moralities?" in *Private and Public Ethics*, ed. Jones, pp. 138, 141. Little is talking not strictly about conscience in this respect but conscientiousness. Little's article is an excellent criticism of Reinhold Niebuhr's argument that there is a sharp distinction between the morality of groups and that of individuals.

43. See, for example, Tom Shaffer and my "Hope Faces Power: Thomas More and the King of England," *Soundings* 61, 4 (Winter 1978): 456-79.

44. That is why appeals to "autonomy" are so unsatisfactory as a basis for why we should be willing to resign from certain tasks and roles rather than cooperate with what we take to be morally doubtful enterprises. See, for example, Edward Weisband and Thomas Franck's account of autonomy in their otherwise fine book, *Resignation in Protest* (New York: Grossman Publishers, 1975), pp. 181-92. For a more satisfying account of what is morally involved in acts of resignation, see James Childress, "Appeals to Conscience," *Ethics* 89, 4 (July, 1979): 315-35.

45. It may seem odd to consider cynicism a virtue at all, but it is certainly one form of disposing our intellectual skills. Moreover, the cynic is formed by profound moral convictions about the nature and centrality of living truthfully and without illusion.

46. There is a close resemblance between patience and suffering, but as Kierkegaard suggests, patience differs from courage as it voluntarily accepts unavoidable suffering. See *Purity of Heart Is To Will One Thing*, tr. Douglas Steere (New York: Harper Torchlights, 1948), p. 173.

47. I would like to thank the Reverend David Burrell, the Reverend Enda McDonagh, and Dr. David Solomon for criticizing an earlier draft of this paper. I owe a special thanks to Anne Hauerwas for attempting to improve the style and to Sara Vaux and Susan Choutka for furthering that effort.

Conclusion

When the court convened at Nurenberg to sift through and pass judgment on the Nazi atrocities, they were faced with the dilemma of establishing whether in fact there were moral reasons why human beings should not exercise on other humans all the power it was within their ability to use. They had to come up with some universally acceptable reasons why those in power ought not do exactly as they pleased with the bodies and minds of other persons. Groups since, grappling with human experimentation or setting up guidelines for research, have come to this wall beyond which certainty is mandated but none seems to appear.

The "laws of humanity" appealed to at Nuremberg, or the Helsinki Guidelines, now form part of the physician's personal code as surely as does the Hippocratic Oath to heal and not harm; yet with burgeoning technology and an increasingly stress-ridden academic and personal existence, the questions still persist. Can we say now as we continue to perfect a range of sophisticated diagnostic tools that we possess adequate moral wisdom to distribute and use these tools? Can we turn to certain fundamental principles, some moral criteria, to guide and judge our actions?

Those moral criteria, it has been suggested in this book, are to be found partially within human nature itself, a nature which unites both function and the humanum, that intrinsic and inalienable yet transcending and sacred dimension of human life. Who is this human person who asserts his powers against the natural universe, against history, and now over against technology, that blessed creation of his own ingenuity? Persons above all are moral beings, existing not only for themselves but in solidarity with their fellows—not only "being" but "being with" in community with other human persons *(mitmenschlichkeit).* A spectrum of views of this person can be sensed as one moves from essay to essay. Some, like Fletcher, lean more to the mathematical in defining the nature and obligations of this person in community, while others, like Kass, savor the mystery of the person. Though Fletcher is exceedingly calculating and Kass profound and metaphysical, their views and those of all the intermediate positions of personhood demand expression in such a volume. And all speak for the dignity and value of the self—that "person" who continually transcends his own biological, functional identity.

The person, then, must not be subjected to the norms of the inanimate world, the world of time and the machine. Because persons are spiritual and moral as well as physical beings, they possess inestimable value and must remain inviolable, even though their bodily functions may be subject to endless technical interventions. The moral criteria that must guide medical treatment are those that are found native to their nature as they seek to know themselves and relate to others in community: both respect and compassion for the other reasoning, feeling, choosing mortal selves whom one confronts.

Leon Kass has set the tone for all the essays that follow his. A life oriented toward quality rather than quantity, being rather that doing, the self rather than the clock, is one in which the powers of the human person flourish. Kass has attacked our obsession with quantity, with physical immortality, suggesting we re-examine the assumptions on which biomedical advance has been based. At some point we must arrest our desperate search for immortality, recognizing that in some ways that search should not be so much for deathlessness as for "wholeness, wisdom, goodness." Such a longing "cannot be answered by prolonging earthly life"—that is, by shoring up, patching up, drawing out bodily *functions.* Rather, it is the *human person,* the unique self, who must wrestle with his mortality. One definition of human "power" as Kass has delineated it appears to be embracing "powerlessness"—accepting our biological limits, loosening our grasp on chronological time in favor of eternal timelessness, a rich present savoring of the life we have now, a life freshened by adopting the perspective of the child: "the natural and eternal renewal of human possibility."

What are our human powers? Like Kass, May has defined "power" in terms of person, not function: a grace to acknowledge "just" respect for the human in another person even when his physical functions are flawed or failing. May pleads for us to "enter into community with the aged," taking them seriously as moral beings. There should be some return to the patriarchal status such persons enjoyed in simpler tribal times before medical science discovered a way to justify the relegation of the older persons to "exceptional disease status" by calling aging a disease and coining the syndrome "Alzheimer's Disease"—senility and senile dementia. As Kass has written, acceptance of our physical limitations makes possible the flourishing of a newly human life. That life encompasses a reassessment of our place in the human community, a place that will include the fit and the unfit, the young and the aged.

Ivan Illich has looked at another facet of our humanity. He calls it subsistence, explaining that he means not just perfection of our physical powers but activation of self-reliance. This means not a dependence upon goods but confidence in one's ability to provide for one's own needs. This kind of health, he says, "cannot be measured quantitatively," but rather constitutes a quality of being in community, an "aliveness of its members in relation to one another." Humanity, then, must be defined in terms of society as well as the individual.

Gaylin has continued to probe the subjective awareness of our own emotional state that marks us as creatures alive to our own powers. "Guilt and its fellow emotions of caring, loving, shame, compassion, empathy, and pity bind us to those who are needed for our own survival," he has stated. Here we probe the implications of saying that "man is a spiritual and moral as well as a physical being"; man thinks, he feels, he acts. He resists being acted upon, and guilt, "the guardian of our goodness," returns in the night to challenge our callous attempts to use others and let ourselves be manipulated. Guilt is a most enlightening feeling, for it yanks us away from complacency and coldness back to some standard of goodness we have deserted. And that standard of goodness, we have been suggesting, lies in the recognition that persons are moral and spiritual as well as physical beings.

Engelhardt believes that reason is the cardinal or unique power which defines our humanity. But he has clarified reason as referring to "persons," that is, beings capable of considered moral choice. Being a person is more than being human, he says, for persons belong to a moral community having the possibility of moral responsibility. "No longer can (human persons) turn to an understanding of their nature qua biological species for a source of moral values. Instead, their destiny is to create and invent their own values." Those values, he suggests, arise from the nature of the person as a thinking, choosing being.

Fletcher's essay has diverged somewhat from the tenor of the other articles in that he wishes to make greater use of mathematics in order to supply fairly the health needs of humans. Building upon the premise that justice is morality, he has advanced a view of justice that would distribute goods and services to all. Fletcher sees the problem as one in which these goods and services are not limitless, however, and therefore fairness of distribution is an essential. Justice as relational, not private, unavoidably embraces triage as inherent in its very nature, that is, "moral obligation ought to take account of differences in persons and differences in circumstances." One of the powers that makes us human is the ability to make carefully considered moral choices of this kind, as Engelhardt and others have advanced.

Where Fletcher, Engelhardt, Illich, and Gaylin dealt with separable facets of human powers (the search for justice, the assertion of rationality and aliveness, and the recognition of feelings), Vaux and Hauerwas, like Kass and May, have explored the human condition as such. Vaux's essay accords deeply with Kass's desire for a rebirth of fresh vision within the accepted limit of our days and May's appeal for a reconstituted community in which the aged are accorded equal moral status. But justice, vitality, rationality, and sensitivity (as those have been given both individual and communal significance) are bound up in hope, as that power which leans the human forward into the future, enabling both his flowering and his care. Moral insight comes to the human person as he is grasped by transcending power—either by hope, that truth which lies beyond in the future, or by God, that infinite being who lies above the person. God thus is the ground of ethics, the force who replaces that which now is with that which will be; he is the power of the future and the transcendence that defines moral reality.

Hauerwas has located the context and contours of the moral impulse by speaking of the value communities within which virtures are inculcated and ethical apperceptions shaped. In an essay summarizing that which has gone before, he has claimed that ethics is not only moral calculation and cost-benefit ratios. It is, of course, this and the rigorous application of natural reason. But fundamentally ethics concerns the deeper currents of value and vision that constitute virtue or vice in the person and community.

All these essays form building blocks in that foundation of ethics we seek to establish to firmly undergird the medical edifice. The stuctural stresses can only be contained and the aesthetic design maintained if these building blocks we have labeled "powers that make us human" are carefully crafted and laid to become the basis of our health care construction.

The essayists have united in asserting the power of the human against attempts to shrink the person to a more manageable collection of physical attributes. If person and function are indeed united, equal, then the stance of the physician must be one of compassion—a careful blending of knowledge and empathy, a refusal to relax this thorny, troubling dialectic into either technical obsession or pre-scientific magical manipulation. "Compassion" defined in the light of these eight essays views science—and knowledge generally—as a divine bequest to empower care and make it efficacious. Recognizing the spiritual and moral dimensions of human persons—and thus of all medical situations—tempers and refines the application of this knowledge, providing a moral frame of reference within which decisions can be made.

Kenneth Vaux

Sara Vaux-Anson

Contributors

H. Tristram Engelhardt, Jr., M.D., Ph.D.; professor of philosophy, Center for Ethics, Medicine, and Public Issues, Baylor College of Medicine, Houston.

Joseph Fletcher, S.T.D, emeritus professor, Episcopal School of Theology, Boston; author of *Situation Ethics*.

Willard Gaylin, M.D.; president, the Hastings Center; psychoanalyst, New York City; professor, Columbia University.

Stanley Hauerwas, Ph.D.; professor of theology, Duke University.

Ivan Illich, Ph.D.; professor, University of Kassel, Kassel, West Germany; director, Center for Intercultural Documentation, Cuernavaca, Mexico; author of *Medical Nemesis*.

Leon Kass, M.D., Ph.D.; Luce Professor of Liberal Arts of Biology, University of Chicago.

William May, Ph.D.; professor of Christian ethics, Southern Methodist University, Dallas.

Kenneth Vaux, Th.D.; associate professor of ethics, University of Illinois College of Medicine in Chicago.